PLCs, DI, & RTI

This book is dedicated to the men we admire most,
the friends who told us to go for it,
our children who supported us with words of encouragement,
each of our parents who modeled for us the importance of education,
teachers who lead and do not accept the status quo,
and
Charlie.

Thank you all; we love you.

A Tapestry
for School Change

PLCs, DI,
& RTI

PROFESSIONAL LEARNING COMMUNITIES
DIFFERENTIATED INSTRUCTION
RESPONSE TO INTERVENTION

JUDY STOEHR   MARIA BANKS   LINDA ALLEN

CORWIN
A SAGE Company

CORWIN
A SAGE Company

FOR INFORMATION:

Corwin
A SAGE Company
2455 Teller Road
Thousand Oaks, California 91320
(800) 233-9936
Fax: (800) 417-2466
www.corwin.com

SAGE Ltd.
1 Oliver's Yard
55 City Road
London EC1Y 1SP
United Kingdom

SAGE India Pvt. Ltd.
B 1/I 1 Mohan Cooperative Industrial Area
Mathura Road, New Delhi 110 044
India

SAGE Asia-Pacific Pte. Ltd.
33 Pekin Street #02-01
Far East Square
Singapore 048763

Acquisitions Editor: Hudson Perigo
Associate Editor: Allison Scott
Editorial Assistant: Lisa Whitney
Production Editor: Cassandra Margaret Seibel
Copy Editor: Cate Huisman
Typesetter: C&M Digitals (P) Ltd.
Proofreader: Jenifer Kooiman
Indexer: Jean Casalegno
Cover Designer: Karine Hovsepian
Permissions Editor: Adele Hutchinson

Printed in the United States of America

Library of Congress Cataloging-in-Publication Data

Stoehr, Judy.

PLCs, DI, & RTI : a tapestry for school change / Judy Stoehr, Maria Banks, Linda Allen.

p. cm.
Includes bibliographical references and index.

ISBN 978-1-4129-9238-1 (pbk.)

1. School improvement programs.
2. Professional learning communities.
3. Individualized instruction.
4. Response to intervention (Learning disabled children)
I. Banks, Maria.
II. Allen, Linda.
III. Title.
IV. Title: PLCs, DI and RTI.

LB2822.8.S74 2011 371.2'07—dc22 2010050206

This book is printed on acid-free paper

11 12 13 14 15 10 9 8 7 6 5 4 3 2 1

Contents

Acknowledgments

We would like to acknowledge the following individuals and groups of people, without whom this book would not have been possible. These individuals and the staffs of these schools, districts, and hotels took time out of their busy lives to listen as we continued our search for the right material. They are old and new friends, teachers, loved ones, and colleagues who inspired, rather than intimidated us, manipulated us, or asked us to go away. They have added value to this text by allowing us to run things by them and be guinea pigs for our journey, and they are successful leaders themselves.

Airport Holiday Inn, Manchester New Hampshire (staff)

Holiday Inn Chicago Midway Airport (staff)

Claudia Lyles

Wissahickon Girl Friends Club

Chris Coyne Kehan

Carol Connard

Souhegan Area Schools

Langston Hughes Elementary

Charles Carroll Barrister Elementary

Fort Thomas Unified School

Jefferson County School

Leland Elementary School

has provided opportunities to extend her knowledge of brain-compatible strategies, of how to build communities of learners, and of teaching students with special needs. Her specialties in brain-compatible learning include how children learn, memory strategies, novelty in the classroom, stress and threat, and processing learning.

Linda is avid about sharing what she has learned from research and from teacher-experts around the country with other teachers. Her slogan has become, "Enriching children's lives by nourishing teachers' minds."

Introduction

The data gathered in *A Nation at Risk* (National Commission on Excellence in Education, 1983) and in the Third International Mathematics and Science study (1995), along with Richard Allington and Sean Walmsley's publication *No Quick Fix: Rethinking Literacy Programs in America's Elementary Schools* (1995), were among the catalysts that propelled the No Child Left Behind (NCLB) mandate that every child will be a reader and a writer by the year 2014. This mandate ushered in a requirement that every school would have a strategic plan in place to ensure that all students would be successful. As an answer to the mandate, innovative ideas such as professional learning communities (PLCs), differentiation of instruction (DI), and response to intervention (RTI) came to the forefront.

It didn't take long for the works of notable individuals such as Howard Gardner, Carol Ann Tomlinson, Heidi Hayes Jacobs, Robert Marzano, and Susan Rosenholtz to gain notoriety, providing insight into students' learning profiles, readiness, and interests and into educators' collaborative discussions. Gardner's theory of multiple intelligences (*Frames of Mind*, 1983) became a vehicle for recognizing and understanding how students learn in a holistic and natural way. His evidence showed that a child might be at very different stages of cognitive development at different times. He believes that students' minds are open to learning and that teachers must develop multiple opportunities for them to investigate and think.

DIFFERENTIATED INSTRUCTION

Carol Ann Tomlinson's first book, *How to Differentiate Instruction in Mixed Ability Classrooms* (1995) followed Gardner's research and offered strategies to meet the needs of all students through differentiation of instruction. Differentiation of instruction is a philosophy that requires educators to shift their thinking pedagogically, with the major focus being on the delivery of new content and skills, providing multiple experiences for students to process the content and skills, and giving students various opportunities to show what they know and can do through time, choice, and voice. This change in paradigm meant that all students would be provided specific plans of instruction that used the four quadrants of the brain—visual, oral, auditory, and kinesthetic. School districts embraced Tomlinson's ideas in large part because they fostered student achievement through differentiated teaching and learning while addressing district mandates in curriculum.

Heidi Hayes Jacobs (2004) enhanced the earlier curriculum mapping work of Fenwick W. English (1999) through a detailed process that focused on assessment, dialogue, reflection, student learning, and the curriculum itself. Mapping enabled teachers to identify redundancies, gaps, and threads in the curriculum both horizontally (within grade levels and across content areas) and vertically (between grade levels) over time. Jacobs's roadmap was a way to look long-range at a unit of instruction and short-range at the immediate lesson within the unit. It included essential questions for the how and the why of the lesson, means for flexible grouping of students, instructional strategies, and diverse approaches to assessment.

To help educators further transform their teaching, Robert J. Marzano wrote *Classroom Instruction That Works* (2001), in which he highlighted nine essential categories of instructional strategies:

1. Identifying similarities and differences

2. Summarizing and note taking

3. Reinforcing effort

4. Homework and practice

5. Nonlinguistic representations

6. Cooperative learning

7. Providing feedback

8. Generating and testing hypotheses

9. Graphic organizers

When combined with Jacobs's mapping of curriculum and Tomlinson's differentiation of instruction, these strategies enhance student thinking and learning.

PROFESSIONAL LEARNING COMMUNITIES

These individuals along with their innovative practices paved the way for adaptations in education that are occurring in the 21st century. As schools began to put differentiation into practice, as they began learning to map their own curricula, as they began to implement research-based instructional strategies, and as they collaborated and reflected on their own practice, they also realized that they needed to spend time discussing how to better implement those changes and how to incorporate the new ideas within the boundaries of their own culture and thinking.

As early as 1989, Susan J. Rosenholtz was hard at work cultivating ideas about key elements of professional learning communities. Her research on improving practice centered on teacher reflection, collaboration, and input. And while delivery, planning, and individual learning profiles became effective means of classroom practice, she recognized that school transformation and improvement were still "owned" by the building administrator. Rosenholtz determined that until there is divergent thinking and shared decision making by teachers, there will be little or no chance for lasting change. Additionally, her research indicates that "teachers with a high sense of their own efficacy are more likely to adapt and adopt new behaviors and more likely to stay in the profession" (Rosenholtz, 1989, p. 74).

Linda Darling-Hammond led the effort to develop national standards for teachers that reflect on what they need to know in order to teach diverse learners. Her work was based on the premise that the better we know our students, the quicker we can intervene in their learning. She summarized it all by saying, "These students need creative and innovative teachers with positive attitudes" (Darling-Hammond & Bransford, 2005, p. 359).

RESPONSE TO INTERVENTION

The Individuals with Disabilities Education Act (IDEA) was reauthorized in 2004 to better meet the needs of students with disabilities through early interventions and services. As schools identify students who are at risk early and intervene in their education quickly, the likelihood of the special education program becoming the dumping ground for difficult-to-educate students is reduced. RTI, a general education initiative written into the reauthorized act, offers educators a framework in which to structure early intervention strategies. At its core, RTI supports students who are at risk by removing barriers to learning.

According to Brown-Chidsey, Bronaugh, and McGraw (2009), "Response to Intervention (RTI) is a roadmap for student success in the general education classroom. It is a wonderful tool you can use to help all of your students especially those who keep you up at night" (p. 1). Mary Howard's *RTI From All Sides* (2009) describes RTI as a "multifaceted way to look at students and make effective, excellent, collaborative plans for literacy instruction" (p. xiii). Its focus is on providing early and effective instruction for students in both academic and behavioral areas.

ABOUT THIS BOOK

This book is written with thoughtful intent to provide educators with the professional knowledge they need regarding DI, RTI, and PLCs. This knowledge will enable them to monitor, adjust, and reflect on current teaching practices and assist them in establishing robust learning communities within schools. It provides answers to the questions, "What's in it for me?" "How is it relevant to my current practice?" "How do I do this when I have so much other stuff on my plate?" and "How do PLC, DI, and RTI fit together?"

The book includes several kinds of resources that educators will find helpful:

- Research and theories supporting PLCs, DI, and RTI
- Examples from the field of education—practical strategies used in K–12 classrooms and examples from our own reflective notebooks
- Collegial conversation guides and protocols for establishing PLCs
- Walk-through checklists and learning-style surveys that are easy to use and educator friendly
- Demonstrations of how to integrate PLCs, DI, and RTI, which—when implemented faithfully over a two- to three-year period—will yield rich and rewarding teaching and learning environments
- An outline of the nonnegotiables of PLCs, DI, and RTI

REFERENCES AND RESOURCES

Allington, R. A., & Walmsley, S. A. (1995). *No Quick Fix: Rethinking Literacy Programs in America's Elementary Schools.* New York: Teachers College Press.

Brown-Chidsey, R., Bronaugh, L., & McGraw, K. (2009). *RTI in the classroom: Guidelines and recipes for success.* New York: Guilford Press.

Darling-Hammond, L. (1997). *The right to learn: A blueprint for creating schools that work.* San Francisco: Jossey-Bass.

Darling-Hammond, L., & Bransford, J. (2005). *Preparing teachers for a changing world: What teachers should learn and be able to do.* San Francisco, CA: Jossey-Bass.

Darling-Hammond, L., & McLaughlin, M. W. (1995, April). Policies that support professional development in an era of reform. *Phi Delta Kappan, 76*(8), 597–604.

English, F. W. (1999). *Deciding to teach and test: Developing, auditing, and aligning the curriculum.* Thousand Oaks, CA: Sage.

Gardner, H. (1983). *Frames of mind: The theory of multple intelligences.* New York: Basic Books.

Hord, S. A. (1994). Staff development change and process: cut from the same cloth. *Issues About Change,* 4(2), 6.

Hord, S. A. (1997). Professional learning communities: What they are and why they are important. *Issues About Change,* 6(1), 8.

Howard, M. (2009). *RTI from all sides: What every teacher needs to know.* Portsmouth, NH: Heinemann.

Jacobs, H. H. (2004). *Getting results with curriculum mapping.* Alexandria, VA: Association for Supervision and Curriculum Development.

Marzano, R. J. (2001). *Classroom instruction that works: research-based strategies for increasing student achievement.* Alexandria, VA: Association for Supervision and Curriculum Development.

Mehring, T. (2001). *Advances in special education.* Bingley, UK: Emerald Group.

National Commission on Excellence in Education. (1983). *A nation at risk: The imperative for educational reform.* Washington, DC: Author.

Rosenholtz, S. (1989). *Teachers' work place: The social organization of schools.* New York: Teachers College Press.

Smith, M. K. (2002, 2008). *Howard Gardner, multiple intelligences and education.* Retrieved from http://www.infed.org/thinkers/gardner.htm

Third International Mathematics and Science Study. (1995). http://timss.bc.edu/timss1995.html

Tomlinson, C. A. (1995). *How to differentiate instruction in mixed ability classrooms.* Alexandria, VA: Association for Supervision and Curriculum Development.

1 Elements and Principles of the Integrated Model

If our teaching is to be an art, we must draw from all we know, feel, and believe in order to create something beautiful.

—Lucy Calkins

It was 110 degrees in Scottsdale, Arizona, when the three of us sat down with a bottle of wine on a shaded patio to talk about the challenges teachers were having implementing professional learning communities (PLC), differentiated instruction (DI), and response to intervention (RTI). In our initial conversation we compared the three elements to objects such as a fork with its three prongs, a set of puzzle pieces that interlock with other pieces, and an umbrella's ribs that support and connect at the crest. But nothing seemed to click until, while researching, we came upon the elements and principles of art.

Our experiences and our discussions led us to believe that teacher buy-in is paramount to effecting change. That's honestly the single most important aspect of learning. We knew from our experiences with educators that we needed to help people connect the three components of this model to something common—something with which they were familiar—in order to understand how everything fits together.

When you read this book, you are going to see that we have adapted the elements and principles of art to help us organize our thoughts and clarify ways the book can be used in school communities. This book is a collaborative work among three colleagues who each have a passion for teaching, and through their discussion, they have learned that they share a common thread: All three of us recognize that not only are many administrators and teachers challenged by PLC, DI, and RTI, they are also at a loss as to how these approaches are interrelated. We would never claim to be experts in all areas of education, but we have been blessed with opportunities to learn from amazing educators around the world, and we have taken the time to locate and apply the best research from experts in education to lay out the *what, why*, and *how* of integrating PLC, DI, and RTI. It is our desire to share those experiences and knowledge with you—our new colleagues.

We visualize this work as an artist views a tapestry, a thoughtful, intentional piece that is aesthetically pleasing in form, texture, and unity. In education, our bottom line is the academic, emotional, and social well-being of our students. The diverse communities in which we work consist of many textures that shape our understanding. The learning spaces and our philosophy regarding pedagogy shape our values and are the threads that bond us in a natural way.

THE FIVE CATEGORIES

In keeping with our "tapestry" theme, we have organized each chapter around five categories: *threads, essence, fabric, design,* and *frame.*

Threads

- What PLC, DI, and RTI are
- The research behind each one
- Who said what about each one, and why she or he said it

Essence

- What's in it for me
- 21st century skills
- Making it rigorous

Fabric

- Defining components of PLC, DI, and RTI
- Walking the walk

Design

- Talking the talk
- How/when to implement

- Why we should integrate it
- How to integrate it

Frame

- Nonnegotiables
- What's in, what's out

Threads

Threads are the filament or group of filaments that make up fabrics. For hundreds of years, they have constituted a way of holding things together to make pieces strong and durable. Threads vary in thickness for different types of sewing. For us, research is the connecting thread, and it has a number of filaments and fibers that change over time. When spun aptly and with integrity, it yields a PLC, DI, or RTI program that can run either independently of the other two or concurrently with them.

Essence

Essence is the nature of a thing. It is what is formulated as universal in the mind and in the language. St. Thomas Aquinas distinguished between an essence and its existence in the fact of its being. His description was later revised to mean that essence is what a person follows from the choices he or she makes. The creation of a tapestry essence includes the choices the artist makes when selecting colors, textures, shapes, and lines. In the field of education, teachers can make informed choices only if they know why they should use particular strategies, programs, and research; how those would work in their classrooms and with particular children; and ultimately how the strategies, programs, or research will affect them personally and professionally. In other words, teachers need the answer to the question, "What's in it for me?"

Fabric

Fabrics are flexible materials consisting of networks of natural or artificial fibers often referred to as thread or yarn. Fabrics appear to be some of the oldest materials in the world. Fabrics have long since been a staple in our society, from keeping us warm to showing our status in society to being used as a form of currency. Properties of fabrics include absorbency, heat conduction, and strength. Fabrics can become softer when washed. They can be creased and folded. Fabrics with poor elasticity can be easily wrinkled; they must be cared for to keep their luster.

PLC, DI, and RTI are analogous to the fabric in our tapestry. Each has a specific purpose and is a staple for the 21st century classroom. They are characterized by flexibility, contextual or natural learning, networking, and when implemented consistently and appropriately strengthen teaching, learning, and leadership.

Design

Design is the groundwork or the basis for creating every object, system, or product. As a process, design can take many forms, depending on what is being designed and who is doing the designing. As a verb, *design* refers to intentionally developing a plan for a product, structure, system, or component. As a noun, *design* refers to a plan that, when implemented, is the basis for a final product. The final product in its broadest sense can be anything from tapestries to websites.

Like design, teaching can take many forms. If the background knowledge, support system, and personal experiences of the educator are insufficient to support it, the focus for teaching can sometimes be too broad. Our PLC, DI, and RTI tapestry model guides teachers and school districts in developing a design that has a narrower focus that is less complicated and more achievable. The intent is to provide a long-lasting and integrated structure that interfaces with existing curricula.

Frame

Frames are enclosures that showcase and/or protect paintings, photographs, pictures, tapestries, or other products. Frames must be selected with care. Some of them are so elaborate that they overshadow the subject matter, while others are nearly undetectable due to the composition of the frames. In some instances the elaborateness of the frame is burdensome and causes the pane of glass shielding the product to shatter, leaving the picture unprotected. With the introduction of digital photo frames in the late 20th century, we were able not only to frame and protect photographs, but also to view them in real time, make editing decisions, and share audio and video clips.

Similarly, some education frameworks are so cumbersome or complicated that they do not serve the needs of teachers and students, or the framework itself overshadows the subject to be taught. This text is formed with the intent to show what it means to be immediately responsive to the needs of teachers and students, providing a framework that serves them and enlightens the subject matter.

WEAVING THE TAPESTRY

Chapters 2, 3, and 4 each address one of the three programs—PLC, DI, and RTI, while Chapter 5 shows how these elements can be combined. Each chapter includes structures and activities to help educators implement the elements, and two appendices provide specific protocols and forms that readers may copy and use in their schools.

In addition, because time, choice, and voice are critical factors in growth and development, and in an effort to ensure there is growth and development for teachers and students, we have developed a list of nonnegotiables for each chapter. These include the following:

- Teacher-student conferring and goal setting
- Teacher-to-teacher shared decision making and problem solving
- Teacher-administrator collaborations, walkthroughs, and feedback
- Analysis and comparison of state and national standards
- Ongoing assessment
- Continuous reflection
- Faithful implementation, with a two- to three-year commitment to the process

These nonnegotiables offer additional connections among PLC, DI, and RTI as educators seek to answer questions such as "What happens in our school when a student does not learn?" and "What happens in our school when a student already knows the material I am teaching?"

REFERENCES

Calkins, L. (1994). *The art of teaching writing.* Portsmouth, NH: Heinemann.

2 Professional Learning Communities

THREADS

There is a deep hunger among faculty members for more meaningful collegial relationships and more "conversational structures" in our institutions.

—Faith Gabelnick

What It Is

The term *professional learning community* (PLC) is based upon the theory that a group of like-minded educators who share common beliefs about teaching and learning come together not only to redefine professional development but also to overhaul their teaching in order to create greater student success. In a PLC, collegial groups are committed to a shared outcome in which both teaching practices and student learning improve. Members of the community work together to create a shared vision, define their beliefs and values, establish teaching and learning goals, and determine objectives to reach those goals. Professional learning communities provide the structure through which educators can plan collaboratively with colleagues to differentiate instruction and provide interventions for students. Because members of PLCs share ideas and concerns, support each other, and are accountable to one another, they typically feel like they are part of a team that helps them to be better informed and more empowered. Additionally, Shirley Hord (1997b) of the Southwest Educational Development Laboratory sees professional learning communities as effective instruments for staff development that can lead to school change and improvement.

The Research Behind It

Discussions about PLCs began in the 1970s around improving workplace behaviors and enhancing teachers' skills and knowledge of emotional intelligence and differentiation. Desired goals were improving student performance, eliminating gaps in performance among different racial groups, providing early intervention, and increasing emotional well-being for all students. At that time, the typical approach to professional development was a one-size-fits-all model, with an administrator determining what was needed and how it would be delivered. What was missing was a two-way dialogue between teachers and administrators to determine what their real needs were and how those needs could best be met. The researchers cited below identified specific priorities for teacher effectiveness, focusing on inquiry, collaboration, and reflection, as well as employing best practices that allow educators to engage as both learners and leaders.

- Durkheim (1979) and French and Raven (1959; Raven, 1992) were pioneers in the influence of work settings who chronicled the study of social integration. They believed that people change their viewpoints and behaviors because of societal impact. Their studies indicated that collaborating with others who seem to be like minded, who have valued skills, or who are authorities in their field presents opportunities for long-term change. They found that the majority influences real changes and that when most of the members of a person's social group have a common belief, that person is apt to adopt it, as well.
- Susan Rosenholtz (1989a, 1989b) determined that the environment in which teachers work has a direct impact on their quality of teaching. She asserted that educators would be more committed and successful if they were encouraged to pursue excellence in their own learning and teaching through collaboration and goal-setting activities with colleagues. She also believed this success would ultimately result in teachers remaining in the profession for a longer period of time. Finally, Rosenholtz concluded that teachers with a strong sense of their own efficacy would be more likely to try new classroom practices.
- Fullan (1991) focused on teachers' work environment as well, and he suggested a change of paradigm, whereby schools would embed continual pursuit of excellence throughout each day. He later

recommended establishing professional learning communities in which teachers and administrators could work together and focus on student achievement. According to Fullan, this focus should incorporate evidence-based curriculum materials, differentiation of instruction, and early intervention and assessment information about student performance.

- Darling-Hammond (1996) named shared decision making as a significant aspect in some schools for reforming curriculum and transforming classroom practice. She found that in those schools where teachers were provided structured collaborative time to plan for and provide instructional interventions, to observe each other's classrooms, and to share feedback, the resulting change was overwhelmingly positive. On the other hand, she noted that teacher workplaces where there was little to no teacher collaboration or shared vision were "embryonic and scattered" (1996, p. 10).

Darling-Hammond determined that the rewriting of the Individuals with Disabilities Education Act provided schools a way to reflect on new ideas regarding Response to Intervention (RTI). Her belief (like those of the authors of this book) was that educators can support each student's learning best when they consider differentiated instruction (DI) in their planning, teaching, and assessing. Instead of teaching prescribed lessons from teacher-proof textbooks, educators should learn about their students' interests, readiness levels, and learner profiles in order to help everyone master content standards.

Although much time and money have been invested in the change process and how to reform educational practices in classrooms, too frequently only rhetorical attention is given to this process. The results are often short-term change efforts that lack the full participation of all school staff. In contrast, creating and supporting a staff's willingness to change will positively impact our students. And, if students are at the heart of why we teach, we must remember several of the old adages that have been passed down over the years—*haste makes waste, look before you leap, stop and think, don't judge a book by its cover.* As Malcolm Gladwell has written, "We believe that we are always better off gathering as much information as possible and spending as much time as possible in deliberation" (2005, pp. 13–14).

Who Said It and Why

Many resources have been published about the effectiveness of professional learning communities. According to Hord, the desired effect of building capacity in the school setting is that the PLC can address changes and demands regarding student achievement, interventions, teacher performance, and accountability (Hord, 1997a). Here is what other resources have said about PLCs:

- Darling-Hammond and McLaughlin (1996) recommend, "Teachers should have opportunities to engage in peer coaching, team planning and teaching, and collaborative research that enables them to construct new means for inquiring into their practice. These occurrences enrich teaching experiences and afford teachers time to share common experiences and adversities" (p. 203).
- "Professional learning communities are organizational arrangements, seen as powerful staff development approaches and a potent strategy for school change and improvement" (Hord, 1997b, p. 3).
- According to Watkins and Marsick (1999), "a centerpiece of reform recommendations is that parents, teachers, administrators, staff members, and students join together to learn their way through change as communities of inquiry and experimentation" (p. 78).

ESSENCE

We have to delve into what is it for the teacher that's going to make this meaningful, and what is it for the student that is going to make this useful?

—Bernice Stafford

In the context of this book, *essence* refers to the physical aspects or attributes of a workplace or to the ongoing growth of persons—their character, their goals, or whatever is most significant for them. Through PLCs, educators ask questions such as, How is it relevant? How is it taking my teaching to the next level? How will this enable me to meet district mandates? The first question many educators ask is, What's in it for me?

What's in It for Me?

The simple answer to this question is that both instructional practices and student performance can be improved through PLCs. Consider these following benefits of working in professional learning communities:

- **Support system.** Educators do not have to do everything alone. Communication and relationships built upon shared problem solving bring about a climate of continuous improvement by individuals who care.

- **Sense of efficacy.** Educators feel valued and realize their contributions, both as teachers and as group members, are significant. They collaborate with their colleagues to determine pedagogy, materials (within parameters set by district resources or state law), and interventions. Teachers and administrators work together to sustain vital aspects of the school's culture.
- **More engaged, motivated, and successful students.** The school shifts to a student-centered format of learning that provides individual pacing through ongoing assessment, flexible grouping, tiering, and curriculum compacting while supporting new habits of mind and making space for students to learn through guided discovery.
- **Focus on what students need academically and behaviorally.** The school promotes a culture for goal setting and reflection that facilitates, supports, and changes the role of the teacher, school administrators, and learners in the classroom. Consequently, teachers are able to respond to students who need multitiered approaches and closely monitored intervention to determine the need for further evidence-based instruction and/or intervention.

Implementation of professional learning communities that focus on both teacher and student needs most often results in a decrease in the dropout rate and an overall improvement in morale. Absenteeism is reduced, both for students and for teachers. And, the achievement gap among students from different backgrounds is decreased, improving the overall academic outcomes in the school.

21st Century Skills

The global economy in which the United States is competing demands innovation, strong thinking and reasoning skills, the ability to work in a team, and technological competence. It is vital that our educational system make parallel changes. In order to fulfill their mission in society, our schools must ready today's students for tomorrow's world beyond the classroom. To be fully prepared, our students need to develop skills in

- critical and creative thinking,
- self-assessment,
- problem solving,
- decision making,
- using real-world tools to achieve high-quality results,

- individual and societal responsibilities,
- teamwork and collaboration,
- higher-order thinking, and
- ways to prioritize, plan, and manage results.

In her text *Rigor is NOT a Four Letter Word* (2008), Blackburn indicates that in order for students to be prepared for the 21st century, DI must be used as a way to strive toward academic and instructional excellence. Blackburn views DI as a way of extending classroom practice into the community so that everyone is engaged in learning. DI techniques provide high-quality instruction and intervention that are designed to meet student needs.

Making It Rigorous

A PLC is often defined as a school in which there is rigor and relevance. The members of the professional learning community continuously pursue learning to heighten their instructional efforts by reflecting on student work, planning for peer learning experiences, designing student-centered investigations, and using data from ongoing assessments. To be rigorous, a lesson must target the higher levels of Bloom's Taxonomy. That lesson is relevant when students are required to use what they are learning to solve real-world issues through open-ended, inquiry-based processes.

Within the structure of PLCs, rigor means that teachers expect all students to learn at high levels. Before beginning each new unit, students are assessed to determine their readiness, they are informed of their expected performance requirements, they see and understand essential questions, and they are made aware of formative and summative assessment criteria. Throughout their learning, they are challenged to create their own meaning and to reflect on how they will apply what they have learned. Through PLCs, teachers can help each other achieve rigor and relevance in their classrooms by incorporating the following:

- Challenging curriculum
- High-level questioning
- Differentiated instruction using resources that target student learning styles and multiple intelligences
- Connections with students' interests
- Strategies that complement expected levels of complexity
- Modifications to instruction as necessary based upon responses from students
- Formative assessments to check for understanding and misunderstandings. (Blackburn & Williamson, 2009)

FABRIC

Nature uses only the longest threads to weave her patterns, so that each small piece of her fabric reveals the organization of the entire tapestry.

—Richard P. Feynman

According to Newmann and Wehlage (1993), "Research suggests that education could benefit substantially from efforts to transform impersonal, fragmented school systems into places where participants share goals and pursue a common agenda of activities through collaborative work that involves constant, personalized contact over a long term" (p. 8).

Walking the Walk

In order to walk the walk of PLCs, educators must have opportunities to network and collaborate with their colleagues, collect and interpret data, employ evidence-based methods and tools, and expand their professional roles and responsibilities. In her studies of workplace conditions, Rosenholtz (1989a, 1989b) determined that in order for teachers to change their classroom behaviors they must be given "time, voice, and choice."

Time, Voice, and Choice

Time, voice, and choice help staff members appreciate diversities and strengths of one another, understand and apply the nuts and bolts of teaching, and document and analyze their roles and responsibilities. PLCs promote results-oriented thinking that is focused on continuous improvement and student learning (Reichstetter, 2006). They provide opportunities for educators to engage in ongoing collegial conversations, receive frequent feedback on their own teaching, and plan with their colleagues. Making choices, setting goals, and maintaining collective inquiry help sustain improvement while strengthening connections among teachers. PLCs also require mutual accountability and, when necessary, change of classroom practices. Conversations about change have become a leading platform for discussions about what really works in schools. In order for change to occur, administrators and teachers must be open in their deliberations, promoting and providing collegial conversations, differentiation in their own learning, and shared leadership.

Time

In PLCs, educators take the time to implant a vision and create an environment for decision making about how and what they teach, as well as ways they can learn together (Leo & Cowan, 2000; Louis & Kruse, 1995; Stoll, Bolam, McMahon, Wallace, & Thomas, 2006). They have time to think about what is needed and why, time to think about what has been taught and how well it worked, and time to consider their own understanding of instructional best practices. Other benefits of providing time include the following:

- Teachers have time to reflect on their practice.
- Support is provided for gradual change, over time.
- Educators are encouraged to take time with their colleagues to examine their own learning, shape practice, and assess progress.

Voice

In PLCs, the collaborative culture provides an environment for teachers to respectfully converse, reflect, and vent. Teachers profit from each other's varied backgrounds and resources (Newmann, 1994), as well as from having a place where they can share their concerns and ideas. Other benefits of providing voice include the following:

- Teachers can express concerns about their own teaching styles.
- Teachers respectfully share observations about growth and development or lack thereof, group interactions, and the perspectives of fellow teachers.
- Teachers feel empowered to communicate thoughts about what they know and need to know about the best ways administrators, fellow teachers, and teacher leaders can make learning possible for a diverse teaching staff.
- Teachers support each other in generating ideas for efficient management and shared decision making.

Choice

In supportive environments, administrators provide opportunities for teachers to share decision making with them and encourage them to assume leadership roles (Hargreaves & Fink, 2006; McREL, 2003). Choices, purposes, and goals of a PLC emerge from the members based on their needs, values, beliefs, and individual or shared experiences (Thompson, Gregg, & Niska, 2004). Increasing teachers' roles and responsibilities enhances their ownership of the choices they make and strengthens their belief in the school's collective ability to shape change. Areas in which teachers may be encouraged to make choices include type and delivery of professional development activities; utilization of resources and personnel;

recommendations of pedagogy, curriculum, and materials; and personal and group goal setting.

The benefits of giving teachers choice include the following:

- An environment is fostered in which teachers take ownership of their school.
- Individuals are empowered to reflect on and manage their professional learning and growth.
- Collaborative instructional opportunities such as team teaching and coteaching become viable options.
- The school environment becomes stronger and healthier.

Through time, voice, and choice, teachers share reflective dialogue, build trust, discover solutions, and successfully address student needs. Long-term benefits of giving teachers time, voice, and choice through PLCs include the following:

- Teacher competence improves.
- Student achievement increases.
- Staff members are generally more trusting, warm, and respectful of their colleagues.
- Teacher longevity is prolonged.
- A stable learning environment is sustainable.

Defining Components

In her publications, Hord (1997b), asserts that schools organized as PLCs are characterized by five dimensions, or components, that are shared by the members of the community:

1. Vision, beliefs, and values

2. Leadership

3. Learning

4. Positive environment

5. Personal practice

Hord asserts that by nurturing, developing, and sharing each piece of the fabric—the five components—and by maintaining a sense of academic rigor with their eyes on students' lives after education, a school staff can evolve into a successful learning community.

Vision, Beliefs, and Values

In a PLC, everyone's focus is on students and learning. Staff understands and is committed to the purpose and goals of the school, and each person understands his or her role in achieving that purpose. They "perceive" what their school will look like at its best and how they will work productively together to make the perception a reality. Staff members with children or grandchildren of their own want them to attend the school at which they work.

In schools where teachers, administrators and staff share vision, beliefs, and values,

- students are asked for input about classroom layout and structure.
- there is a familial sense that is characterized by statements such as, "this is *our* school" and "we are all in this together."
- teachers recognize that students vary in background knowledge, readiness, language, preferences in the ways they learn, and interests.
- the school communicates with the public by sharing examples of high-quality achievement and learning through the school newsletter, in the newspaper, on the school cable television channel, on the school's website, and through school events.

Leadership

Administrators and faculty members share power and authority for making decisions and solving problems. Teachers are encouraged to take leadership roles. Group mentality and cliques among individuals or groups are replaced with a culture of collaboration. Administrators model collegiality with their teachers; they learn together and talk about teaching and leading. Teaching is no longer viewed as a solitary job behind a closed door. Teachers share their craft and knowledge of teaching via on-the-job demonstrations and observations. Educators root for one another's success.

In schools where shared and supportive leadership exist,

- building and district administrators participate in professional development.
- administrators and teachers use the words *we* and *us* rather than *you* and *they.*
- meetings are not bogged down with items best left for administrative council or e-mail.
- teachers have a say in the process or next steps.
- teachers, administrators, and community members regularly go on "Teacher to Teacher Walk-Throughs" (see Appendix B) to collect data and reflect on their practice.

Learning

Members of the learning community determine what they must learn and how they will learn it in order to address students' needs. Administrators and teachers from all grade levels, subjects, and job descriptions meet regularly to study together and work collaboratively. A common vocabulary is established around teaching and learning. Protocols are used for discussion. Evidence-based teaching practices and lessons are studied and modeled. Learning occurs through differentiation, data analysis, conversation, intervention, and problem solving. It is continuous and focuses on ways to better serve diverse learners through new instructional strategies, revisions of the curriculum, and use of regulations, standards, and policies. Teachers incorporate new learning into their lesson plans and activities. After implementing new strategies, teachers debrief together and revise the strategies as necessary.

In schools where collective learning and its application are evident,

- continuous goal setting and reflection occur.
- educators use evidence-based practices for talking in a way that shows they take accountability. They use protocols such as "Partner Talk," "Talking Points," or "Symphony" (see Appendix B) to promote conversation, and they model these types of communication explicitly in the classroom setting.
- academic language is the norm, and educators use the language of teaching and learning with students to build stronger vocabularies.

Positive Environment

An environment that supports PLCs includes aspects such as structure and organization, personnel interactions and relationships, and instructional leadership and resources. Structural and organizational factors provide for the physical requirements of PLCs, such as time and place. Members need both time and a place to meet for community building and team work, to respond to surveys and needs assessments, and to reflect on data gathered through teaching and learning experiences. (A sample Professional Learning Communities Survey and a Needs Assessment for Differentiated Professional Development are provided in Appendix A.) Frequent gatherings are scheduled during which extensive conversations, goal setting, and questioning occur. These consistent schedules and supportive structures reduce teacher isolation, encourage professional learning and collaboration, and provide opportunities to determine what is working and what is not.

Continuity provides opportunities for members of PLCs to cultivate commitment, both to the organization and to each other. Interpersonal development flourishes in professional learning partnerships in which there are attitudes of respect, openness, and caring among group members. Peer confidence is built when school communities engage in trust-building activities that allow all community members to get to know each other in a positive way on a personal level.

Building administrators can model a caring environment and demonstrate commitment to the PLC through instructional leadership. The role of the instructional leader within a PLC must be one in which the priority is to encourage student and teacher growth. By becoming a part of the professional learning community and helping provide meaningful opportunities for teachers to meet, question, collaborate, and define meaningful learning activities for students, administrators defy the top-down leadership approach.

In schools that provide a positive environment,

- trust-building activities occur regularly.
- policies are planned and developed that foster collaboration.
- focus groups are created based on professional needs.
- assessments and surveys are developed collaboratively to determine teacher knowledge, needs, and self-efficacy.

Personal Practice

Community members give and receive feedback that supports their professional growth. Teachers visit each other's classrooms on a regular basis to provide a different lens on teaching and learning. This is followed with immediate feedback and thoughtful questions that often generate proactive problem solving. When teachers come together as peer coaches in a nonthreatening manner, they share personal reflections and protocols that may support the implementation of new practices. As the building administrator supports a culture of thinking, learning, collaborative problem solving, and shared leadership, he or she models congenial, trusting relationships among staff. In this type of environment, teachers are comfortable sharing both their successes and their failures. They praise and recognize one another's triumphs and offer empathy and support for each other's troubles.

In schools that support shared personal practice,

- teachers learn the purposes of collaborative discussions, protocols, and lesson studies through continuous application.
- grade-level conversations occur regularly. Agendas and dates are set in advance. The focus is on improving student attitudes, aptitudes, and behaviors. Collegial discussions go beyond the three B's: belly-aching, begging, and blah, blah, blah.

- peer coaching and collaboration are the norm. If teachers don't understand a new practice or academic vocabulary, they feel comfortable seeking the support of a fellow teacher, administrator, or community member.
- building administrative teams are members of PLCs and recognize the high degree of trust needed for teachers/colleagues to share willingly in such a setting.
- principals willingly provide instructional leadership through mentoring, live lesson demonstrations, peer coaching, or outside consultation for support.

DESIGN

To put it as succinctly as possible, if you want to change and improve the climate and outcomes of schooling, both for students and teachers, there are features of the school culture that have to be changed, and if they are not changed your well-intentioned efforts will be defeated.

—Seymour Sarason

A common practice for preparing a garment for preview in the field of design is to use glue. However, repeated changes and adjustments made to the garment wear away the glue, and it begins to disintegrate. The fabric then has to be basted. Conversely, when the proper threads are used to hold the fabric together through basting, the simple act of pushing, pulling, and weaving with the needle creates a design that is suggestive of a continuous pattern that is evenly supported.

In the same way, the thread, essence, and fabric of a PLC must be woven together to create a school culture that is truly a learning community. To accomplish this, the members of the PLC must continually and thoughtfully guide its direction, monitor its progress, and evaluate its overall effectiveness.

Talking the Talk

Effective PLCs require "talk"—communication and collegiality. This "talk" must help teachers find a common language while they are building collegiality. It must also be accountable. Classroom teachers often use *accountable talk* as a way to increase comprehension and build community in classrooms. In a PLC, accountable talk may be used to support or challenge the theories of others, to confirm that the information being presented is accurate, to press for explanation, or to interpret and clarify student work. Accountable talk follows established norms of good reasoning, employs reasonable evidence, and supports critical and creative thinking. Accountable talk provides the following:

- Accountability to the PLC ("I agree with my colleague regarding curriculum-based . . . because. . . .")
- Accountability to knowledge ("Where did that term *pedagogy* come from? I don't know what it means.")
- Accountability to rigor and reasoning ("So, by sharing this piece of student work, you are showing how you were providing and monitoring intervention over a period of . . . ?")

A positive school culture reflects norms of common purpose, accountability, and collegial continuous inquiry. PLCs must use accountable talk to create environments in which teachers can trust and talk to one another. Appendix B includes three protocols PLCs can use for accountable *talk:* "Partner Talk," "Symphony," and "Talking Points."

Sharing ideas, concerns, and thoughts with others is vital to learning. Accountable talk nourishes and supports learning. Teachers and school systems who engage in this evidence-based practice model responsible behavior that is an important part of an effective thinking and learning community. Over time, teachers can learn to use accountable talk in PLCs during protocols, as well as in the classroom with their own students.

Using Protocols

A protocol is a structure used by groups such as PLCs to achieve deep understanding about teaching and learning through in-depth, insightful conversations. The focus is typically on improving teacher performance and increasing student achievement through research-based practices such as differentiated instruction and interventions. It is an evidence-based approach to discussion that promotes active listening and reflection, as well as a decrease in isolation of individual participants. Everyone agrees upon and follows the guidelines for conversation in order to make the environment safe and the discussion nonthreatening.

Protocols have different structures that reflect their individual purposes. For example, some emphasize explanation, others evaluative feedback or reflection. In addition, teachers and administrators can adapt protocols for use in the classroom or restructure protocols for use during professional dialogues. Appendix B includes the following protocols that are useful for facilitating conversations in PLCs: "Bull's-Eye," "Looking Back," "R.I.C.E.," "Silhouette," "Teacher to Teacher Walk-Through," and "Tools of the Trade."

Using protocols provides members of PLCs the opportunity to build trust by thinking, working, and learning together. They also ensure that there is some equity in terms of how each member's concerns or needs are addressed. Protocols give teachers a license to listen and make the most of the limited time educators have to engage in professional conversations. The presenter has the opportunity to describe an issue, reflect on personal learning, or address a concern. He or she has the option of either asking or being asked thought-provoking questions, seeking peer coaching, or exploring differing perspectives.

How and When to Begin a PLC

Schools must begin transforming themselves by looking first at what teachers and students need to learn and be able to do in the 21st century. In order to integrate teacher planning for professional development into district-level planning, educators must reflect about their practice via efficacy surveys. This planning should include meeting with colleagues in small groups in order to work out a thorough format that will include comprehensive, user-friendly steps for implementation of PLCs.

The following checklist includes suggested steps to follow when setting up a PLC:

- Determine your school's need of and readiness for change—identify possible barriers.
- Find others who share your vision—begin with an exchange of ideas.
- Structure a framework—build from the ground up.
- Consider a small starting point for change—something visible or exterior, such as redecorating the office or front hallway of the school.

Prior to setting up the PLC, teachers should complete assessments about their schoolwide culture. Small groups can then discuss the responses in a nonthreatening manner, thus promoting the structure of PLCs. From the discussions, information and insights that will focus on learning can be shared. Two templates are provided in Appendix A: the "Evaluation for Teacher Effectiveness," which assesses how effective teachers feel they are in general, and the "Teacher Survey about Writing," which assesses how educators feel about teaching writing. In addition, the following list of online survey tools may help schools begin their discussions about improvement in teaching and learning:

- Survey Share: www.surveyshare.com
- Vista Survey: www.vista-survey.com

- New Zealand Council for Educational Research: www.nzcer.org.nz/default.php?products_id=2251
- Survey Monkey: www.surveymonkey.com/

Surveys and checklists, such as those mentioned above, and the "Teacher to Teacher Walk-Through" protocol (referred to earlier in this chapter) help teachers and administrators to develop goals and conversations that relate to school mission statements. The "Teacher to Teacher Walk-Through" protocol assists school communities in discussing teaching and learning, developing a common language for educational systems, and looking at trends in teaching and learning. Information obtained through "Teacher to Teacher Walk-Throughs" can be used to set goals for improvement of practice or to verify that existing best practices are already in use.

During the initial stages of the PLC, teachers work in teams with colleagues who share a common interest. They set individual and group learning goals, and determine how they will provide updates about their learning journey to the school community.

In the ensuing months, team membership can remain voluntary but may be expanded based on personal needs and individual buy-in. During this capacity building stage, schools can begin calling teams "learning communities." Team members can be sent to PLC institutes such as those offered by the National Staff Development Council, the American Society for Curriculum and Development, or the Choice Literacy Institute. External consultants can be hired as coaches for each team as needed.

Team participation can remain voluntary in coming months, but teams should eventually organize goals that are embedded in shared ideas, content-based topics, and action research, such as that of Calhoun (1994). Some type of data should be presented as evidence of improvement, effectiveness, or learning. Data on student learning may be gathered from standardized tests, districtwide curriculum-based assessments, student work samples, portfolios, and other sources. The processes of data analysis and goal development typically determine the content of teachers' professional learning talks in the areas of instruction, curriculum, and assessment.

Benefits of analyzing data include the following:

- Informing instructional decisions
- Identifying students who are at risk
- Determining interventions for specific students
- Evaluating effectiveness of existing programs
- Providing information about the relevance of mission and vision

- Revealing a clear direction for goal setting
- Monitoring, adjusting, and closing existing gaps in achievement

Following are some tips for organizing and sustaining PLCs:

1. **Take baby steps.** Begin setting goals. Discuss, reflect, and share with others to determine how to proceed. Consider and reflect on the following:
   - What principles motivate my/our practice?
   - How can I/we get started acquiring new knowledge?
   - What design will I/we use to validate evidence of significant learning?

2. **Plan cooperatively.** Group team members with common needs to determine what information is needed to proceed. Involve all team members in developing a topic or issue to study and the process to be used. Follow up with analysis—perhaps of a lesson delivery or of an assessment outcome—and discuss the findings.

3. **Set high expectations.** Explore a variety of proposals, get responses from team members, and prioritize next steps. Investigate ways to pursue and achieve excellence, including the following:
   - Test assumptions related to teaching after long-term modeling has been provided.
   - Provide coaching sessions focused on classroom implementation and the analysis of teaching.
   - Allow time for struggling teachers to observe classroom practice of those who have created successful learning environments.

4. **Start small.** Tackle one initiative at a time. Implement the initial plan with a small group so that modifications can be made as necessary before introducing it to everyone else.

5. **Study and use the data.** Examine the results of the initial implementation and reflect on the results to objectively determine whether the plan should be kept, revised, or discarded.

6. **Plan for success.** Learn from the past, improve on or reject things that did not work, and then move on. Future success or failure depends on existing attitudes and behavior.

7. **Go public.** Once the plan has experienced initial success, invite others to become involved. Celebrate and share small successes.

8. **Exercise the body and nourish the brain.** There is a strong connection between movement and learning (Jensen, 2005). Take turns

leading simple movement activities and providing brain teasers for the group. Additionally, provide healthy food and beverage choices, including water, during meetings.

Specifics of PLC Meetings

A PLC begins with educators who are dedicated to learning and improving practice. PLCs from individual schools can combine with others within and across districts to form communities that include teachers and administrators, support staff, central office personnel, school board members, parents, and business partners.

PLCs focus on improving teaching practice and student achievement. They use data from a variety of sources to ascertain the strengths and needs of teachers and students in order to find ways to close both teaching and learning gaps. Specific actions may include the following:

- Book study (a protocol for this activity, "Teacher Book Discussion Groups," appears in Appendix B)
- Data analysis
- Review of student work
- Review of teacher work
- Curriculum alignment

PLC meeting times and frequency should be set by the group members. Meeting agendas include reviewing current student information and progress, setting goals, determining whether identified actions and interventions are making a difference, studying and discussing new ideas and strategies, and identifying other professional learning needs to support school-wide success. Figures 2.1 and 2.2 show sample agendas for actual PLC meetings.

Figure 2.1 School A PLC Agenda

School A PLC Agenda
April 9, 2010
Critical Friends Group

1. If I had a . . . [choose and illustrate a tool that most reflects your work ethic].
2. Protocol Reminders

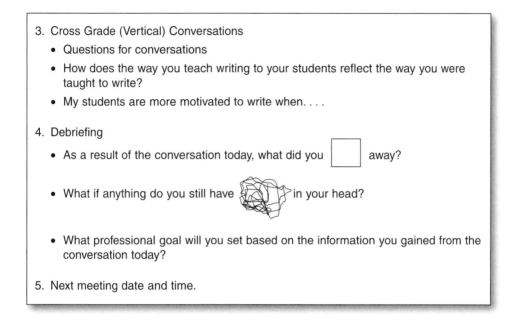

3. Cross Grade (Vertical) Conversations
   - Questions for conversations
   - How does the way you teach writing to your students reflect the way you were taught to write?
   - My students are more motivated to write when. . . .

4. Debriefing
   - As a result of the conversation today, what did you ☐ away?

   - What if anything do you still have 🌀 in your head?

   - What professional goal will you set based on the information you gained from the conversation today?

5. Next meeting date and time.

Figure 2.2 School B PLC Agenda

School B PLC Agenda
August 11, 2007

1. 'Walk and Talk" activity

2. Introduction and overview of session

3. K-W-L (know-want-learn) activity about data informing instruction

4. PowerPoint presentation

5. Teacher attitude survey about feelings, attitudes, and belief systems regarding change, data, teaching, and learning. The results of the survey will provide the PLC with information that can be used to discuss data and improve individual practice.

6. Changing practice: a discussion about what practices teachers can improve and how

7. Review of session: some things to consider

8. Exit ticket—a quick written assessment of the knowledge and understanding the participant has of the session just completed

9. Individual goal setting

A recommended starting activity for a PLC is "Walk and Talk" in Appendix B.

Possible discussion ideas for PLC meetings include the following:

- Strategies and activities for differentiating instruction and interventions
- Tips and tricks of the trade
- Data discussions to develop school or student improvement plans
- Evaluation of instructional materials or practices
- Alignment of instructional practices with state or national standards
- Examination of teacher or student work
- Lesson studies
- Designing curriculum-based assessments
- Analysis of protocols used during PLC meetings
- Exploration of technology- and media-related teaching and assessment tools

It is recommended that PLCs regularly build in time for teachers to discuss ideas and strategies with each other. From time to time, a coach or consultant may be brought in to share new research and its potential effect on the school's students. In addition, PLC meetings should include these items:

- Meeting data, such as member attendance, topics discussed, prior actions taken
- Meeting format (protocols)
- Agenda
- Record keeping (PLC log)

Goals for PLCs

In *Learning by Doing: A Handbook for Professional Learning Communities at Work* (2006, pp. 2–4), Dufour, Dufour, Eaker, and Many state that the goals for PLCs should be to focus on positive results for all regarding learning and to discover strengths and weaknesses in teaching in order to learn from one another. Commitment to both the professional growth of teachers and the learning needs of students results in a culture that is likely to achieve successful school reform.

Earlier in this chapter, several long-term benefits of giving teachers time, voice, and choice through PLCs were listed. They merit being restated as goals worth pursuing:

1. **Teacher competence will improve.** Through open and honest conversations about their practice, collaborative problem solving, effective professional development, accountability, and increasing their understanding about teaching and learning, all teachers will continually become better and better.

2. **Student achievement will increase.** As teachers improve their abilities to make data-based decisions that are standards driven, their planning, instruction, and assessment will change to meet the needs of their students. This will directly impact the success of all learners.

3. **Staff members will become generally more trusting, warm, and respectful of their colleagues.** As PLC participants develop collegial relationships with each other, they become less guarded and more willing to openly share issues, ideas, and concerns. This sets the stage for transformation throughout the entire learning culture.

4. **Teacher longevity will be prolonged.** Teachers who like what they are doing, feel valued and respected, and see positive results from their efforts are much more apt to stay in the profession and at a particular school. They build relationships with each other and their students, creating consistency and continuity.

5. **A stable learning environment will be sustainable.** Adults who share a common vision, along with beliefs and values that support their work, are able to focus their energies on achieving goals—both for their students and for themselves.

Organizing PLCs

PLCs can be organized into a variety of different types of cadres, groups, or teams, each with a different purpose or focus. Some of those are listed in Table 2.1, along with a possible focus of each.

Table 2.1 Types of PLCs

Type	Focus
Teacher partnerships	Improving specific teaching strategies
Grade-level teams	Coordinating planning and instruction
Content-area teams	Improving curriculum
Vertical teams	Aligning expectations and student experiences
Whole school	Innovative teaching and learning
Cross district	Operational and equity issues

FRAME

Teaching is reminding others that they know just as well as you. You are all learners, doers and teachers.

—Richard Bach

The framework that supports the PLC is the teacher. These framers assemble major structural elements, including personnel—such as students, administrators, and others—and evidence-based practices, such as DI, RTI, and, of course, PLCs. When properly joined or linked, the structure is protected and supported. Without order, sense, and the proper tools, the pieces of the frame do not fit together, and thus the frame becomes weak.

Nonnegotiables

The nonnegotiables for building a successful PLC are listed under "What's In" in Table 2.2. Items listed under "What's Out" must be eliminated if the structure is to endure.

Table 2.2 What's In—What's Out

What's In	What's Out
• Time, voice, and choice • Beginning conversations with colleagues about change • Identifying a problem • Differentiating professional learning • Group roles and responsibilities • Looking closely for evidence of change in practice • Peer coaching and collaborating • Long-range planning • Year-long focus • Unpacking state and national standards with colleagues • Nurturing and supportive environment • High-quality, evidence-based practices • Collecting and reflecting	• Planning from the top down • Mandating who must participate • District-mandated goals • Multiple initiatives to accomplish in a year • One-size-fits-all inservice trainings • Administrators leading change • Buying a packaged program • High expectations only for the teachers who are "in" • One-year mentoring programs • Managing through fear and power

Chapters 3 and 4 of this book, along with the publications and organizations listed in Appendix C, will help your PLC identify and explore the interrelationships among professional learning communities, differentiation of instruction, and response to intervention in order to create a tapestry for school change.

REFERENCES AND RESOURCES

Annenberg Institute for School Reform. (2004). *Professional development strategies that improve instruction.* Providence, RI: Author.

Banks, J. A. (2003). Multicultural education: Characteristics and goals. In J. A. Banks (Ed.), *Multicultural education: Issues and perspectives* (4th ed.), pp. 3–30. New York, NY: Wiley.

Bernhardt, V. (1998). *Data analysis for comprehensive school wide improvement.* Larchmont, NY: Eye on Education.

Beyond the Book. (n.d.). *Professional learning communities boost math scores.* Retrieved from http://www.beyond-the-book.com/successstories/success_053106.html

Blackburn, B. A. (2008). *Rigor is not a four-letter word.* Larchmont, NY: Eye on Education.

Blackburn, B. A., & Williamson, R. (2009). The characteristics of a rigorous classroom. *Instructional Leader, 22*(6), 1–3.

Blythe, T., Allen, D., & Powell, B. S. (1999). *Looking together at student work: A companion guide to assessing student learning.* New York, NY: Teachers College Press.

Bolam, R., McMahon, A., Stoll, L., Thomas, S., & Wallace, M. (2005). *Creating and sustaining effective professional learning communities.* Retrieved from http://www.dcsf.gov.uk/research/data/uploadfiles/RB637.pdf

Boyd, V. (1992). *School context. Bridge or barrier to change?* Austin, TX: Southwest Educational Development Laboratory.

Boyd, V., & Hord, S. M. (1994, April). *Principals and the new paradigm: Schools as learning communities.* Paper presented at the annual meeting of the American Educational Research Association, New Orleans, LA.

Buffum, A., & Hinman, C. (2006). Communities: Reigniting passion and purpose. *Leadership, 35*(5), 16–19. Retrieved from http://www.allthingsplc.info/articles/articles.php

Burnette, B. (2002). How we formed our community. *Journal of Staff Development, 23*(1), 51–54.

Caine, G., & Caine, R. N. (2000). The learning community as a foundation for developing teacher leaders. *NASSP Bulletin, 84*(616), 7–14.

Calhoun, E. (1994). *How to use action research in the self-renewing school.* Alexandria, VA: Association for Supervision and Curriculum Development.

Carmichael, L. (1982). Leaders as learners: A possible dream. *Educational Leadership, 40*(1), 58–59.

Coburn, C., & Russell, J. (2008). Getting the most out of professional learning communities and coaching: Promoting interactions that support instructional

improvement. *Learning Policy Brief, 1*(3), 1–5. Retrieved from http://www
.learningpolicycenter.org/data/briefs/LPC%20Brief_June%202008_Final.pdf

Cowan, D., & Leo, T. (1999). Launching professional learning communities:
Beginning actions. *Issues About Change, 8*(2), 1–8.

Darling-Hammond, L. (1993). Reframing the school reform agenda. *Phi Delta
Kappan, 74*(10), 752–761.

Darling-Hammond, L. (1996). The quiet revolution: Rethinking teacher development. *Educational Leadership, 53*(6), 4–10.

Darling-Hammond, L., & McLaughlin, M. (1996). Policies that support profes-
sional development in an era of reform. In M. McLaughlin & I. Oberman
(Eds.), *Teacher learning: New policies, new practices* (pp. 202–218). New York, NY:
Teachers College Press.

Drucker, P. (1985). *Innovation and entrepreneurship: Practice and principles.* New York,
NY: Harper & Row.

DuFour, R. (2003). Building a professional learning community: For system leaders, it means allowing autonomy within defined parameters. *The School
Administrator.* Retrieved from http://findarticles.com/p/articles/mi_m0JSD/
is_5_60/ai_101173944

DuFour, R. (2004). What is a professional learning community? *Educational Leadership,
61*(8), 6–11.

DuFour, R., DuFour, R., Eaker, R., & Many, T. (2006). *Learning by doing: A handbook
for professional learning communities at work.* Bloomington, IN: Solution Tree.

DuFour, R., & Eaker, R. (1998). *Professional learning communities at work: Best prac-
tices for enhancing student achievement.* Bloomington, IN: National Education
Service, and Alexandria, VA: Association for Supervision and Curriculum
Development.

Durkheim, E. (1979). *Suicide.* New York, NY: Free Press.

Eaker, R., & Gonzalez, D. (2006). Leading in professional learning communities.
National Forum of Educational Administration and Supervision Journal, 24(1), 6–13.

Fawcett, G. (1996). Moving another big desk. *Journal of Staff Development, 17*(1),
34–36.

Feger, S., & Arruda, E. (2008). *Professional learning communities: Key themes from the
literature.* Providence, RI: The Education Alliance, Brown University.

Feynman, R. P. (1985). *Surely you're joking, Mr. Feynman.* Reading: New York, NY:
Norton.

French, J. R. P., Jr., & Raven, B. (1959). The bases of social power. In D. Cartwright (Ed.),
Studies in social power (pp. 150–167). Ann Arbor, MI: Institute for Social
Research.

Fullan, M., with S. Stiegelbauer. (1991). *The new meaning of educational change* (2nd ed.).
New York, NY: Teachers College Press.

Gabelnick, F., MacGregor, J., Matthews, R., & Smith, B. (1990). *Learning communities:
Creating connections among students, faculty, and disciplines.* San Francisco:
Jossey-Bass.

Gladwell, M. (2005). *Blink: The power of thinking without thinking.* New York, NY:
Little, Brown.

Haar, J. M. (2003). Providing professional development and team approaches to
guidance. *Rural Educator, 25*(1), 30–35.

Hargreaves, A., & Fink, D. (2006). Redistributed leadership for sustainable professional learning communities. *Journal of School Leadership, 16*, 550–565.

Hinman, C. (2007). Developing a substantive professional learning community. *National Forum of Educational Administration and Supervision Journal, 24*(1), 29–35.

Hord, S. (1997a). *Professional learning communities: Communities of continuous inquiry and improvement.* Austin, TX: Southwest Educational Development Laboratory. Retrieved from http://www.sedl.org/pubs/catalog/items/cha34.html

Hord, S. (1997b). *Professional learning communities: What are they and why are they important?* Austin, TX: Southwest Educational Development Laboratory. Retrieved from http://www.sedl.org/change/issues/issues61.html

Hord, S., & Rutherford, W. L. (1998). Creating a professional learning community: Cottonwood Creek School. *Issues About Change, 6*(2), 1–8.

Huffman, J. B. (2000). One school's experience as a professional learning community. *Planning and Changing, 31*(1 & 2), 84–94.

Huffman, J. B. (2003). The role of shared values and vision in creating professional learning communities. *NASSP Bulletin, 87,* 21–34.

Huffman, J. B., Hipp, K. A., Pankake, A. M., & Moller, G. (2001). Professional learning communities: Leadership, purposeful decision making, and job-embedded staff development. *Journal of School Leadership, 10*(5), 448–463.

Huffman, J. B., Pankake, A., & Munoz, A. (2007). The tri-level model in action: Site, district, and state plans for school accountability in increasing school success. *Journal of School Leadership, 16*(5), 569–582.

Hughes, T. A., & Kritsonis, W. A. (2007). *Professional learning communities and the positive effects on achievement: A national agenda for school improvement.* Retrieved from http://www.allthingsplc.info/pdf/articles/plcandthepositiveeffects.pdf

Isaacson, N., & Bamburg, J. (1992). Can schools become learning organizations? *Educational Leadership, 50*(3), 42–44.

Jensen, E. (2005). *Teaching with the brain in mind* (2nd ed.). Alexandria, VA: Association of Supervision and Curriculum Development.

Jessie, L. G. (2007). The elements of a professional learning community. *Leadership Compass, 5*(2). Retrieved from http://www.naesp.org/resources/2/Leadership_Compass/2007/LC2007v5n2a4.pdf

Kleine-Kracht, P. A. (1993). The principal in a community of learning. *Journal of School Leadership, 3*(4), 391–399.

Kruse, S., Louis, K. S., & Bryk, A. (1994). Building professional community in schools. *Issues in Restructuring Schools, 6,* 3–6. Retrieved from http://www.wcer.wisc.edu/archive/cors/Issues_in_Restructuring_Schools/ISSUES_NO_6_SPRING_1994.pdf

Leo, T., & Cowan, D. (2000). Launching professional learning communities: Beginning actions. *Issues About Change, 8*(1) 1–16. Retrieved from http://www.sedl.org/change/issues/issues81/issues-8.1.pdf

Literacy and Numeracy Secretariat, Province of Ontario. (n.d.). *Professional learning communities: A model for Ontario schools.* Retrieved from http://www.edu.gov.on.ca/eng/literacynumeracy/inspire/research/PLC.pdf

Little, J. W. (1989). Norms of collegiality and experimentation: Workplace conditions of school success. *American Educational Research Journal, 19*(3), 325–340.

Little, J. W. (2003). Inside teacher community: Representations of classroom practice. *Teachers College Board, 105*(6), 913–945.

Louis, K. S. (2006). Changing the culture of schools: Professional community, organizational learning, and trust. *Journal of School Leadership, 16*(5), 477–489.

Louis, K. S., & Kruse, D. (1995). Professionalism and community: Perspectives on reforming urban schools. Thousand Oaks, CA: Corwin.

Louis, K. S., Marks, H. M., & Kruse, S. (1994). *Teachers' professional community in restructuring schools.* Madison, WI: Wisconsin Center for Educational Research, University of Wisconsin–Madison. ERIC Document Reproduction Service No. ED31871. Retrieved from http://eric.ed.gov

Lyon, L. (1994). Professional community: Three case studies. *Issues in Restructuring Schools, 6,* 7–16. Retrieved from http://www.wcer.wisc.edu/archive/cors/Issues_in_Restructuring_Schools/ISSUES_NO_6_SPRING_1994.pdf

Martin-Kniep, G. O. (2004). *Developing learning communities through teacher expertise.* Thousand Oaks, CA: Corwin.

McLaughlin, M. W., & Talbert, J. E. (1993). *Contexts that matter for teaching and learning.* Stanford, CA: Center for Research on the Context of Secondary School Teaching, Stanford University.

Mid-continent Research for Education and Learning (McREL). (2003). *Sustaining school improvement: Professional learning community.* Retrieved from http://www.mcrel.org/pdf/leadershiporganizationdevelopment/5031TG_proflrncommfolio.pdf

Mitchell, C., & Sackney, L. (2006). Building schools, building people: The school principal's role in leading a learning community. *Journal of School Leadership, 16,* 627–640.

Moller, G. (2006). Teacher leadership emerges within professional learning communities. *Journal of School Leadership, 16,* 520–533.

Murphy, C. (1997). Finding time for faculties to study together. *Journal of Staff Development, 18*(3), 29–32.

Newcomb, A. (2003). Peter Senge on organizational learning. *School Administrator, 60*(5), 20–25.

Newmann, F. M. (1994). School-wide professional community. *Issues in Restructuring Schools, 6,* 1–2. Retrieved from http://www.wcer.wisc.edu/archive/cors/Issues_in_Restructuring_Schools/ISSUES_NO_6_SPRING_1994.pdf

Newmann, F. M., & Wehlage, G. (April, 1993). Five standards of authentic instruction. *Educational Leadership, 50*(7), 8–12.

Olivier, D. F., & Hipp. K. (2006). Leadership capacity and collective efficiency: Interacting to sustain student learning in a professional learning community. *Journal of School Leadership, 16,* 505–519.

O'Neil, J. (1995). On schools as learning organizations: A conversation with Peter Senge. *Educational Leadership, 52*(7), 20–23.

Phillips, J. (2003). Powerful learning: Creating learning communities in urban school reform. *Journal of Curriculum and Supervision, 18*(3), 240–258.

Prestine, N. A. (1993). Extending the essential schools metaphor: Principal as enabler. *Journal of School Leadership, 3*(4), 356–379.

Protheroe, N. (2008). Developing your school as a professional learning community. *NAESP Research Roundup.* Retrieved from http://www.naesp.org/ContentLoad.do?content Id=1094

Raven, B. (1992). A power/interaction model of interpersonal influence: French and Raven thirty years later. *Journal of Social Behavior and Personality, 7,* 217–244.

Reichstetter, R. (2006). Defining a professional learning community: A literature review. *E&R Research Alert,* 06.05. Retrieved from http://www.wcpss.net/evaluation-research/reports/2006/0605plc_lit_review.pdf

Rentfro, E. R. (Winter, 2007). Professional learning communities impact student success. *Leadership Compass, 5*(2). Retrieved from http://www.naesp.org/resources/2/Leadership_Compass/2007/LC2007v5n2a3.pdf

Rosenholtz, S. J. (1989a). *Teacher's workplace: The social organization of schools.* New York, NY: Longman.

Rosenholtz, S. J. (1989b). Workplace conditions that affect teacher quality and commitment: Implications for teacher induction programs. *The Elementary School Journal, 89*(4), 421–439.

Senge, P. (1990). *The fifth discipline: The art and practice of the learning organization.* New York, NY: Currency Doubleday.

Senge, P. (1995). On schools as learning organizations: A conversation with Peter Senge. *Educational Leadership, 52*(7), 20–23.

Sergiovanni, T. J. (1994a). *Building community in schools.* San Francisco, CA: Jossey-Bass.

Sergiovanni, T J. (1994b). Organizations or communities? Changing the metaphor changes the theory. *Educational Administration Quarterly, 30*(2), 214–226.

Siver, D. (2005). *Drumming to the beat of different marchers, grades K–12.* Nashville, TN: Incentive.

Spears, J. D., & Oliver, J. P. (1996, April). *Rural school reform: Creating a community of learners.* Paper presented at the annual meeting of the American Education Research Association, New York, NY.

Stoll, L., Bolam, R., McMahon, A., Thomas, S., Wallace, M., Greenwood, A., & Hawkey, K. (2005). *What is a professional learning community? A summary.* Retrieved from http://www.decs.sa.gov.au/docs/documents/1/Professional LeaningComm-1.pdf

Stoll, L., Bolam, R., McMahon, A., Wallace, M., & Thomas, S. (2006). Professional learning communities: A review of the literature. *Journal of Educational Change, 7*(4), 221–258.

Stoll, L., & Louis, K. S. (2007). Professional learning communities: Elaborating new approaches. In L. Stoll & K. S. Louis (Eds.), *Professional learning communities: Divergence, depth, and dilemmas,* pp. 1–14. Berkshire, UK: Open University Press.

Strahan, D. (2003). Promoting a collaborative professional culture in three elementary schools that have beaten the odds. *The Elementary School Journal, 104*(2), 127–146.

Supovitz, J. A. (2002). Developing communities of instructional practice. *Teachers College Board, 104*(8), 1591–1626.

Supovitz, J. A., & Christman, J. B. (2003). Developing communities of instructional practice: Lessons from Cincinnati and Philadelphia. *CPRE Policy Briefs,* RB-39. Retrieved from http://www.cpre.org/images/stories/cpre_pdfs/rb39.pdf

Sykes, G. (1996). Reform of and as professional development. *Phi Delta Kappan, 77*(7), 465–476.

Thompson, S. C., Gregg, L., & Niska, J. M. (2004). Professional learning communities, leadership, and student learning. *Research in Middle Level Education Online, 28*(1), 1–15. Retrieved from http://www.nmsa.org/Publications/RMLEOnline/Articles/Vol28No1Article2/tabid/439/Default.aspx

Tomlinson, C. A. (1995). *How to differentiate instruction in mixed-ability classrooms.* Alexandria, VA: Association for Supervision and Curriculum Development.

Tomlinson, C. A., & Eidson, C. C. (2003a). *Differentiation in practice: A resource guide for differentiating curriculum, grades K–5.* Alexandria, VA: Association for Supervision and Curriculum Development.

Tomlinson, C. A., & Eidson, C. C. (2003b). *Differentiation in practice: A resource guide for differentiating curriculum, grades 6–12.* Alexandria, VA: Association for Supervision and Curriculum Development.

Tucker, C. (2008). *Implementing and sustaining professional learning communities in support of student learning.* Alexandria, VA: Educational Research Service.

U.S. Department of Education, Office of Elementary and Secondary Education. (2002). *No Child Left Behind: A desktop reference.* Washington, DC: Author.

Vescio, V., Ross, D., & Adams, A. (2006, January). *Review of research on professional learning communities: What do we know?* Paper presented at the NSRF Research Forum, Denver. Retrieved from http://www.nsrfharmony.org/research.vescio_ross_adams.pdf

Watkins, K. E., & Marsick, V. J. (1999). Sculpting the learning community: New forms of working and organizing. *NASSP Bulletin, 83*(604), 78–87.

Wells, C., & Feun, L. (2007). Implementation of learning community principles: A study of six high schools. *NASSP Bulletin, 91*(2), 141–160.

White, S. H., & McIntosh, J. (2007). Data delivers a wake-up call. *Journal of Staff Development, 28*(2), 30–35.

Wignall, R. (1992, June). *Building a collaborative school culture: A case study of one woman in the principalship.* Paper presented at the European Conference on Educational Research, Enschede, the Netherlands.

Williams, R., Brien, K., Sprague, C., & Sullivan, G. (2008). Professional learning communities: Developing a school-level readiness instrument. *Canadian Journal of Educational Administration and Policy, 74*(6). Retrieved from http://umanitoba.ca/publications/cjeap/articles/illiamsspraguesullivanbrien.html

3 Differentiated Instruction

THREADS

We only learn by doing if we reflect on what we have done.

—John Dewey

What It Is

Differentiation is a teaching philosophy that incorporates a variety of research and brain-based strategies, ideas, and activities. It is a collection of focused, student-centered instructional plans that allow learners to take different paths to eventually reach the same goal. A differentiated classroom has as its hallmark diversity—in student learners (their readiness, interests, and learning styles), in instruction and assessment tools, in the multiple ways to group students based on purposes of assigned tasks, and in the cache of management tools that keep kids safe and secure while learning and that keep the room organized while learning flows easily.

Teachers in a differentiated classroom pay attention to the environment, the physical setting, and the emotional states that drive the learner. Are the students in a state of apathy, or boredom, or excitement, or confusion? Eric Jensen (2003) explains that teachers have the power to direct the emotional conditions of their students that will optimize learning. This ability of the teacher to influence learning states is quite remarkable, and also important. Teachers in the differentiated classroom help students recognize their ability to manage their own learning states. A differentiated classroom also requires that both teachers and students understand how students learn. As teachers stay current on the implications of brain research and use that knowledge to create a more efficient and learning-filled classroom, it is important that they also share that information with students, so the students can understand the best methods to take content and skills to long-term memory.

Just as artists have a variety of media through which to represent their ideas, teachers have a variety of educational media from which to choose to represent learning in multiple ways. We chose a tapestry to represent differentiated instruction (DI), response to intervention (RTI), and professional learning communities (PLCs), as we see all the components woven and intertwined to create an amazing piece of learning. The fibers of differentiation alone are varied, colorful, and unique and could create a beautiful stand-alone piece, but joined with the other two components covered in this book, they will make a more beautiful and transformational whole.

The Research Behind It

The idea behind differentiation comes from the understanding that our classrooms are places that house a variety of active learners who deserve to have support and planning for their education. Carol Tomlinson (2003) suggests that students need differentiation especially when they

- have given up on their own learning or have been given up on by their family and school associates. They may be seen as "unmotivated" but need someone to help them change that state.
- have come to the school with English as a second (or third) language and are struggling to understand critical components of everyday life as well as the critical components of a state-mandated curriculum.
- have come to school with more than a basic understanding of the curriculum, a wide range of life experiences, and high motivation or capability; that is, they are ready to integrate more than the standards or curriculum requires. When that challenge in learning is lacking, students act out or make inappropriate choices.
- have come to school with less than a basic understanding of the curriculum and have limited experiences with life beyond their most immediate community. They struggle with encoding and retrieving information as easily as their peers. They may need additional support through varied approaches, additional time, or collaboration with peers.

In examining the research behind the value of knowing our students better, we always include readiness, interest, and learning profiles. Patricia

Wolfe (2001) and David Sousa (2001) both discuss the importance of using the term *readiness* to describe how a student's learning ability changes over time; their concept varies with fixed concepts of IQ and ability. Teachers who are aware of their students' varying states of readiness are able to provide instruction for both large and small groups of students. They educate students at or slightly above instructional levels, taking into account the mixed abilities of students, and present challenges without causing frustration, confusion, or resignation.

Who Said It and Why

Tomlinson used the term *differentiation* in her book *The Differentiated Classroom: Responding to the Needs of All Learners* (1999), and the educational world seemed to have a new mantra. Many people have since redesigned her model and set requirements for one part or another to fit their understanding of differentiated instruction, but much of the model falls close to what Tomlinson laid out in her book. There aren't rules to DI, but there are some guidelines amidst all of this educational jargon that truly help to make this philosophy a more natural part of our classrooms.

In the late 1950s, individuals such as Ken and Yetta Goodman were discussing programs designed for grouping students of differing abilities (Dreeben & Barr, 1988). The practice took hold in the 1980s, and the term *ability grouping* seemed to encompass all that we refer to as differentiation of instruction. In reality, students were assessed and grouped by their reading or mathematics abilities, and lessons to suit the needs of the students in each group were planned.

Allington (1983) described a different instruction, rather than differentiation of instruction, that occurred within grouping arrangements. Teachers spent time with groups, providing instruction in the area of word attack and comprehension. Students who were capable moved at a faster pace and were exposed to varied activities. Students who struggled to retain information were seldom afforded opportunities to move at a faster pace or explore concepts independently. As a result, the use of ability grouping came under fire.

Whole language and *guided reading*, structured frameworks that unfolded in the late 1980s, paved the way for differentiation of instruction. These formats, as cited by Constance Weaver (1988) and Ralph Peterson (1992), used systematic assessment, monitoring, and adjustment to determine the needs of students. Since that time, small-group instruction has become widely used within a literacy framework (Fountas & Pinnell, 1996).

Today, authors and researchers such as Carol Tomlinson, Constance Weaver, and Ralph Peterson continue to show us how connections between *what* is being taught and the *way* it is taught impact the whole child. The thoughts behind their works include the following:

- Be open with students about their own learning processes.
- Move away from product-driven teaching.
- Allow students time, choice, and voice in the learning journey.
- Ensure intervention through differentiated teaching.

ESSENCE

> *The illiterate of the 21st century will not be those who cannot read and write, but those who cannot learn, unlearn, and relearn.*
>
> —Alvin Toffler

Our classrooms today are exceptionally diverse in so many ways. We have students of various family and historical cultures, religious and political backgrounds, and economic statuses. They have differing life experiences, background knowledge, learning strengths and disadvantages, and even different levels of motivation to learn. Teachers skilled in the philosophy and instructional strategies of DI will have the best chance to move students forward socially, emotionally, and academically regardless of the amazing diversity within the classroom, and sometimes *because* of that diversity.

Law does not mandate DI. It does not have specific rules or time lines, only guidelines. But all students deserve to move forward academically, socially, and emotionally, and because they have the right to end up farther along the educational continuum than anyone thought they could, differentiation becomes a moral and ethical mandate.

What's in It for Me?

When teachers are first introduced to DI, they are often overwhelmed by the amount of planning they perceive will be required of them. Even though they recognize the potential advantages for their students, they must be convinced that the learner outcomes are worth the teacher effort. The following four responses address their question of "What's in it for me?"

- **Support system.** The aspects of time, choice, and voice (addressed in Chapter 2) provide teachers with greater insights about themselves and their colleagues. For DI to be successful, teachers cannot think and work in a vacuum. When they talk, plan, and even teach together, they soon learn that shared responsibility is less stressful and more productive than going solo.

- **Sense of efficacy.** Success breeds success. When teachers see their students succeed, they feel successful. This results in higher self-confidence and a willingness to continue exploring more ways to differentiate instruction and assessment.
- **Students more engaged, motivated, and successful.** In the differentiated classroom, students are actively engaged in hands-on learning that is both respectful and relevant. By teaching content standards in multiple ways, teachers are able to stimulate students' thinking and guide their learning.
- **Focus on what students need academically and behaviorally.** Through the use of research-based strategies and tools, teachers have a better sense of academic and behavioral management within their classrooms. By learning about their students' interests, readiness, and learner profiles, teachers can target what students need through the ways in which they learn best.

21st Century Skills

Twenty-first century skills are woven into and throughout a differentiated classroom. Technology is an obvious part of that thread, as it is such an element of children's everyday existence. Students need to be able to do more than listen to a lecture, design a slide presentation, or use a computer to practice skills. The world of work demands a larger understanding, not just keyboard processing skills. Higher-order thinking, creative and innovative thinking, and communication and collaboration are some of the skills seen as necessary for students as suggested by the Framework for 21st Century Learning designed by the Partnership for 21st Century Skills (2004).

Making It Rigorous

Experts such as Barbara Blackburn suggest there is a rigor gap, and that one of the ways we can close it is by incorporating differentiated instruction. Blackburn (2008) asserts that by raising our expectations of all learners, by increasing their engagement in the classroom, by providing complexity of learning and thinking tasks, and by making meaning through relevance, we can begin to close the rigor gap. To ensure that teaching and learning are rigorous, schools must

- assess the current degree of rigor and relevance in educators' teaching.
- establish professional development communities that are teacher driven and results oriented.

- focus on high expectations with improvement in planning, instruction, and assessment.
- use data to determine the growth of teaching and learning in the school community.

According to Blackburn (2008), there are several practices that support rigor. Many schools have begun using walk-through checklists, teacher efficacy surveys, and evidence-of-rigor forms for measuring progress in closing the rigor gap. (Appendix A includes several forms that can be used for these purposes.) The following are some evidence-based practices that teachers can use to close the rigor gap:

- Helping students understand *why* what they are learning is important and *how* it affects them
- Asking open-ended questions
- Incorporating inquiry-based teaching and learning
- Facilitating student conferences and goal setting
- Fostering curiosity and lifelong learning by providing students opportunities to explore learning that is personally relevant

Appendix A includes a form called "Measuring Rigor" to help you reflect on the extent of rigor in your lesson.

FABRIC

We may exhibit an admirable command of content, and possess a dazzling variety of pedagogical skills, but without knowing what's going on in our students' heads, that knowledge may be presented and that skill exercised in a vacuum of misunderstanding.

—Stephen Brookfield

Depending on the educator, writer, researcher, or presenter to whom you listen or whom you read, you will notice there are many varying thoughts on what the components of differentiation are. Some experts focus on one piece and leave out another, while others demand that differentiation be defined within a very narrow scope. Just as there are differences in how children learn, there are differences in what people consider the salient definition or concept of differentiation. We believe that one of the most important threads that runs through all of our fabric is that when working with each component of a differentiated classroom, the teachers must have the intention of moving a child forward from where he or she is academically, socially, and emotionally.

Differentiation is not haphazard. It is not pulling a book off a shelf and looking up a best teaching strategy, then using it because it sounds good. Every part of a differentiated classroom is planned so that at the end of the day, the week, the lesson, the chapter, or the unit, the picture is one of success—both for the students and the teacher.

Walking the Walk

In this chapter we point out the most important of the well-known components of DI and show how they can be used most effectively with RTI and PLCs to make a positive change in the learning profiles of students. We frame all of these choices in instruction with the teacher's conscious intent. We use instruction in its broadest form to include anything that influences how a student changes his or her learning—from the teacher's instruction, assessment, and climate of the class to class grouping, tiering, and what we know about how children learn.

Defining Components

One of the first and best ideas in DI is that a teacher should be conscious of every student's unique personal story and through those stories set up a positive classroom environment. There are so many ways to learn how each child accesses new information, makes sense and meaning of the new learning, is able to retrieve the information for assessment, takes on leadership roles, and learns the tenets of good discipline. The tools used to glean this information are widely distributed and created by innovative educators everywhere:

- interest inventories—both those assessing students' content knowledge and others more general in nature
- inventories that assess multiple intelligences and learning styles
- leadership profiles
- student and parent conversations
- observations of students' behaviors
- anecdotal information regarding their learning preferences, skills, interests, and so forth

Some of these tools are more subjective than others, and students are able to manipulate them to some degree. However, valid and useful information can be gleaned through most of them. Appendix A includes an Interest and Learning Profile Inventory to use with middle and high school students.

Setting up a Positive Classroom Environment

When teachers envision the learning environment of the classroom, they often think in terms of the physical space. Following are some ideas about the organization and aesthetics of the classroom:

- six spaces and places for literacy, based on the research of Debbie Diller (2008), including well-organized areas for whole group and small group reading instruction, classroom libraries, literacy work-stations, teacher desks, and storage areas
- a variety of seating based on the needs of particular students, e.g., easily distracted students, students who need a working partner more often, students who enjoy working independently
- walls painted in softer shades
- multiple types of lighting from natural, full spectrum, and incandescent sources
- plants in the environment
- room temperature between 68 °F and 72 °F for optimal comfort
- plenty of ventilation and fresh air
- frequently changing bulletin boards, displays, and materials that include much student-generated work
- materials and manipulatives for student use within student reach
- organization that makes materials easy to locate

Several other aspects of the learning environment, management issues, and teaching procedures must also be addressed. These include the following:

- Classroom procedures and routines
  o collecting and distributing materials
  o lining up to leave the classroom
  o attaining and using hall passes
  o listening to announcements
  o planning for late arrivals
  o planning for student absences
  o seeking permission to leave for the restroom
  o asking permission to access the water fountain
  o being prepared during the instructional periods
- Student expectations
  o knowing what conversation levels should be during various teaching times, such as whole group, small group, and independent learning times
  o knowing how to get help during instructional times

- knowing what participation during class looks and sounds like
- knowing exactly what is required from an assignment or task— what it should look like when completed and where the completed work should be placed
- knowing the classroom behavior guidelines, rules, and consequences
- knowing how to support other class members using positive praises and phrases
• Teaching procedures and routines
- breaking a topic into chunks and teaching it step by step
- teaching a topic using visual, auditory, and kinesthetic techniques
- assessing before, during, and at the end of every unit
- practicing and rehearsing
- processing
- reinforcing
- reviewing periodically

Tomlinson includes another component that definitely affects the learning environment. In *Fulfilling the Promise of the Differentiated Classroom* (2003), she mentions learning the "mood" of the classroom as being key. In *Tools of Engagement: Managing Learner States for Learner Success* (2003), Eric Jensen shares strategies to engage students through respect, relationship, and hope. He asserts that by paying attention to the emotional states of our students, we can better manage their behavior and learning. Some of the components of classroom mood on which both Jensen and Tomlinson agree might include the following:

- balance of seriousness and celebration
- perseverance regarding work instead of a feeling of drudgery
- sense of respect for all students rather than favoritism
- shared responsibility among students and teachers
- plentiful opportunities for social interaction
- evidence of established routines and rituals
- environment free of stress and threat

There are several good sources teachers can use when setting up a classroom environment for learning. Dr. Becky Bailey's "conscious discipline" is a classroom management program and a socioemotional curriculum that is based on current brain research, child development information, and developmentally appropriate practices. Dr. Bailey's book is also called *Conscious Discipline* (2001). Rick Smith's book *Conscious Classroom Management: Unlocking the Secrets of Great Teaching* (2004) is a good source for some of the basic "invisible" skills of setting up a classroom management program. He offers many practical tips within his work, and his constant reminder of "procedure before content" is a wonderful way to look at the beginning of any instructional or behavioral plan.

Other good management systems are available as well. In order to create a classroom that is free of stresses and threats, teachers should consider using a program that is based on teaching children internal controls as opposed to rule-bound power structures that require the frequent use of negative feedback or completing a task "because the teacher said so."

Use of Flexible Grouping

Flexible grouping is a significant factor in classroom management. It gives students opportunities to process new content with a variety of other students over a period of time; to brainstorm ideas, thoughts, and solutions with a heterogeneous mix of students; to design research projects with students having similar interests; or to get additional help on specific skills. Flexible grouping provides the teacher a multitude of options when deciding the best way to group students for particular assignments.

Sometimes the best option is for heterogeneous pairs or small groups of students to gather quickly for a short amount of time to discuss a question posed by the teacher or a new idea drawn from the text or the lecture just completed. After such a three- or four-minute discussion, the conversations are debriefed by the teacher with the whole class. Through this class discussion, misconceptions are cleared up, and additions to the information are delivered or processed.

From time to time students with similar needs are brought together in small groups or with partners. Through a formative assessment tool such as "Ticket Into Class," these students may have shown confusion or misunderstanding on a similar skill or concept. Data gathered through RTI universal screenings or ongoing formative assessments give constant rise to such changing flexible groups based on instructional need. These homogeneous groups stay together only as long as it takes the students to learn the needed skill or content.

Tomlinson (2001) encourages the use of a variety of grouping strategies so that students don't see themselves as lifelong members of one group or another. It is within these small, temporary groups that students receive direct teacher instruction and interventions to boost their abilities with specific skills and to process new content in order to take ownership of the new information. In the past, some students seemed to always belong to the upper echelon known as the bluebirds or the redbirds. Struggling students were often permanent members of the buzzard group. No longer are they permanently relegated to a low-performance group. They move through skill groups with different children and are frequently in groups with higher-performing students. As soon as individual students reach mastery of specific skills and content, they are moved into other groups, where they work on different or more complex skills and content.

Below are some appropriate activities for homogeneous grouping:

- Drill and practice
- Math computation
- Studying for a recall-type test
- Answering comprehension questions
- Investigations or independent studies

Periodically students are placed together in interest groups to explore new topics and content relationships.

According to Gregory and Chapman (2002), cooperative learning within small heterogeneous interest groups promotes the use of higher-level thinking skills as they discuss a common topic or question. When students collaborate on projects in which they investigate an idea or a question, it is important for each student to have a designated role within the group. Each student needs to understand his or her role and what the responsibilities of that role require.

There should be a respectable and appropriate role for each person in the group, and each time the group meets, each person should quickly voice what his or her job will entail for that assignment. This procedure keeps group members on task and more responsible for the end project. As Rick Smith (2004) suggests in his chapter "Procedure Before Content," teach group protocol just as you would teach the structure for any other instructional task.

Flexible groups may consist of pairs, triads, or more than three students, depending upon the activity, the purpose of the grouping, and the individual makeup of the group. Some students are simply not able or ready to work in a group larger than two or three. And while others may enjoy being in a group of four or five, the teacher must be on the lookout for "hitchhikers"—those students who let the other team members do all the work. Some types of flexible groups are listed in Table 3.1, along with the purpose they may serve.

Flexible grouping allows the teacher the opportunity to assess both the academic abilities and the behavior of individual students in an ongoing fashion. The students also learn to self-assess based both on criteria that

Table 3.1 Types of Flexible Groups

Type of Group	Purpose
Interest	Find similarities among students
Random	Process or collaborate before or after a lesson
Homogeneous	Focus on similar skills or knowledge levels
Multiple intelligences	Learn about and appreciate each other's strengths
Heterogeneous	Learn from each other's diverse background and perspective
Cooperative	Assume specific roles and responsibilities

the teacher teaches and models and on the examples of academic work and behavior provided by fellow students. Below are some of the benefits of flexible grouping:

- Meeting the needs of all students
- Explicit and systematic instruction
- Opportunities for practice and responding
- Instructional materials matched to student ability
- Instant corrective and appropriate feedback

Strategies and Activities for Differentiating Content

To differentiate content, the teacher presents new content and skills in multiple ways. Each time the content is delivered through a different pathway, a student has another opportunity for exposure to that new information, helping him or her to actually make meaning from the material. Some students who were unable to access the content through a lecture might work with a small group to access the need-to-know information. Others may require seeing the content in a more visual way, through graphic organizers, diagrams, videos, or other approaches. Still others may want to read and reread the text and their notes to absorb the basic information the first time. Additionally, some students may need to use a more kinesthetic method of accessing the new material, either independently or in small groups.

Students access information in a variety of ways and often in several ways for the same material. Some of the options for differentiating content are listed in the sections that follow.

Concrete Approaches

Students who learn best through concrete approaches access information through direct experience by using one or more of the five senses or through the multiple intelligences. Examples include the following:

- Manipulatives
  - globes and maps
  - math manipulatives
  - various manipulatives and tools for specific content areas, for example, balances, scales, and weights
  - specific concrete objects used to explain abstract ideas of particular content areas
- Activities
  - lab experiments and field experiences
  - field trips
  - activities with peer and adult mentors to assist in learning
  - additional experiences at interest workstations
- Teaching strategies
  - Preteach vocabulary words before reading in a content area text (up to two weeks prior for struggling students)
  - Activate prior knowledge in the content areas before the unit of study begins, for example, with the use of bulletin boards, word walls, conversations, picture books, and photographs
  - Deliver content in sequential chunks (teach a chunk, assess a chunk)

Problem-based learning (PBL) and inquiry learning are two other concrete approaches that use strategies from several categories, such as accessing content, processing the new content, and completing a product. PBL and inquiry learning embody representational strategies as well as the concrete, abstract, and technological aspects. PBL encourages cooperative groups of students to solve teacher-designed simulated real-world problems. Under the direction of the teacher, students determine the problem, identify the variables, explore possible solutions, and develop a way to ultimately solve the problem. Through PBL, students restructure their own knowledge and understanding using a variety of resources and then present their findings to an audience.

Inquiry learning stems from a curiosity-based approach. Similar to PBL, it focuses on questioning and critical thinking, as well as problem solving. Students design the research question based on the standards unit being taught, and the research results in a product that relates information to the audience and causes discussion and reflection.

Representational Approaches

Students who learn best through representational approaches access information by depicting the new concept through nonlinguistic methods, such as drawing, role-playing, and using manipulatives. The focus of the representational approach is not on words. In fact, it uses few or no words, and includes the following examples:

- graphic organizers, for example, pie graphs, bar graphs, T-charts, Venn diagrams, and story boards
- charts and graphs to communicate information visually, for example, a graph to show the average price of gasoline over a period of time, a chart that shows a specific portion of the periodic table, or a graph that shows the number and types of pets in each student's home
- use of events and interests in students' lives as examples in content areas

Abstract Approaches

Students who learn best through abstract approaches access information through higher-level thinking skills, such as observation, analysis, and evaluation. Examples include the following:

- use of student goal setting as a weekly good habit
- provision to set a purpose for the learning by the teacher or student
- use of multiple text and resource materials, when possible, at varying degrees of challenge or reading levels
- keying the need-to-know concepts and bold-facing priority vocabulary
- use of "I wonder" statements to deepen and extend the current learning and foster curiosity within content
- use of a big-picture concept as well as step-by-step understanding within each unit of study

Technology- and Media-Related Approaches

Students who learn best through technology- and media-related approaches access content through various types of media. Following are some suggestions:

- interactive media, e.g., SMART Boards, Promethean boards, blogs, WebQuests, media exclusively used by the teacher or other students for presentations of new content
- music equipment

- virtual field trips online, for example, those provided by the National Zoo, the Metropolitan Museum of Art, and TeacherTube
- research, using blogs and wikis, for information to use in responding to reading, science, or social studies experiences, or in critiquing movies, restaurants, tourist sites, etc.
- multimedia presentations, including PowerPoint presentations created by the classroom teacher or online teacher cohorts
- audio and video streaming clips purchased through a licensing program by the school for classroom use
- ideas presented through a variety of modalities, e.g., student presentations of researched material on standards-based questions related to the unit topics, or songs presented from websites such as www.Songs4Teachers.com, where content is taught through quick and easy lyrics
- use of text-to-speech software (e.g., Read & Write Gold) so that students can access content that is difficult to read but is understandable when they hear that content read aloud electronically

Strategies and Activities for Differentiating Process

Differentiating process is an intentional procedure of offering multiple opportunities to students to make sense and meaning of the new content and skills that have been delivered to them or accessed by them. David Sousa, in *How the Brain Learns* (2006), reminds us of the principal difference between sense and meaning. New information that is easily understood by a learner is said to make sense, whereas when the new information can be or is connected to past experiences for the learner, it then has meaning. For example, students can listen to a lecture, see a video, do an experiment, or access new information in a variety of ways, and through this initial learning of the content, the new information seems to be understood by the students—it makes sense! But for those students who cannot make a connection from that new learning to something in their past learning, even in the recent past, the new information isn't likely to be stored permanently. The more often new skills and content are processed, the better chance the student has of making connections.

Since the new content and skills may have been delivered by the teacher or accessed by the students in a variety of ways, it follows that students need diverse ways to make sense of it. Processing can occur formally through writing, talking, drawing, or manipulating the new information. Approaches to processing include targeting the multiple intelligences (MI) and learning styles in order to offer options for practice, rehearsal, understanding, and extension of the new learning. In the lower grades, teachers will need to spend more time explaining, teaching, and modeling how the multiple intelligences are used to process new information, but as the students have more experiences with a variety of MI activities, they should need less hand holding as they are offered choices.

Often in middle and high school, the teacher-preferred method of having students process information is note-taking, even though not all students are good at copying notes from the board, overhead projector, or SMART Board. Note-taking is a type of processing, but it is effective only when students are taught how to go back into the notes and match them to their graphic organizers, how to underline the most important of information, how to find priority vocabulary words, how to restate the information in a more concise form, and how and why it is connected to their own lives—that is, how it is meaningful and relevant to their learning. If the students do not make sense or meaning of their note-taking, what alternative (or differentiated approach) to processing can be offered to those students who need to understand the content that has been delivered? Where do they go from here?

It is during processing that information begins to encode itself in our brains in a more complete way. The more ways we manipulate the information, the better chance we have of its moving from the working table of memory to long-term memory. For example, body memory is the best memory we have. If we learn something with our hands, or through the movement in a dance or an action, then we have a much better chance of retrieving that information than if we just read it or see it. Having students stand up, move a few feet away from their desks, get a partner, and share new information is an easy way to get them to process socially through body memory. When students have processed and encoded information and skills through multiple pathways, they will be prepared to reclaim the information stored for any type of assessment, whether it is formal or informal. Even if they can't remember the information from a past lecture, they have stored it another way. Following are some of the options for differentiating process:

Concrete Approaches

Students who learn best through concrete approaches process information through direct experience with the new content by using one or more of the five senses or through the multiple intelligences.

- Manipulatives
  - materials that lend themselves to exploration using the multiple intelligences and learning styles, especially considering auditory, visual, and kinesthetic modes of learning

- globes and maps
- math manipulatives, for example, tiles, cubes, geoboards, dice, and counters
- virtual manipulatives, such as Promethean and SMART boards
- various manipulatives and tools for specific content areas, for example, balances, scales, and weights
- specific concrete objects associated with particular content areas used to explain abstract ideas
- Activities
  - lab experiments and field experiences after the delivery of content to give students time to make sense of the abstract information
  - activities with peer and adult mentors to assist in learning
  - activities using interest workstations for additional exploration
  - writing simulations, plays, and Readers' Theaters
- Teaching strategies
  - Give students opportunities to turn to a neighboring student and explain a just-learned concept.
  - Vary the pacing based on students' abilities to make sense and meaning of the information, giving them ample opportunities for practice and rehearsal.
  - Group students in ways that expose them to the perspectives of others.
  - Design anchor activities and workstations that contain respectful, appropriate tasks for each level of student based on individual readiness, interest, and learning profile.
  - Make sure students understand expectations for the academic task, the cooperative task if that is part of the assignment, and the behavior. The degree of structure that is required will vary according to each student's independent work habits. At the end of each week, students should be able to self-assess for academic and behavioral progress.

Representational Approaches

Students who learn best through representational approaches process information by making sense and meaning of the new concept through a nonlinguistic method with few or no words, such as drawing, role playing, and using manipulatives. Examples include the following:

- Use graphic organizers such as time lines, concept maps, semantic word maps, and unit organizers to assist students in visualizing the big picture of the new learning.

- Use charts and graphs to communicate information visually, for example, to show student-collected data or information to be shared.
- Use events and interests in students' lives as examples in content areas such as history, religion, economics, celebrations, geography, education, climate, literature, art, and language structure.
- Have students create nonlinguistic representations such as doodles, drawings, diagrams, graphics, and small pictures with course notes. For instance, if it helps the student to draw a mnemonic out to the side of the new vocabulary word, then he or she should create that drawing. If a quick time line with graphics to represent events helps with the notes that were taken, then that is appropriate as well. Sometimes sketching facial expressions near notes will help a student remember something particular that was said or felt about a specific event, person, or idea.
- Teach students to recognize the patterns within the skill and the content—these may or may not be nonlinguistic patterns. It is usually easy to identify the patterns we see in mathematics, but what about the patterns that are found in nature, in the way we set up desks in the room, or the way that cause and effect is so predictable? The brain seeks patterns and it often helps the learner make sense of new learning when it begins to fit in a recognizable pattern.

Abstract Approaches

Students who learn best through abstract approaches process information through higher-level thinking skills, such as observation, analysis, and evaluation.

- Manipulatives
  - additional resource materials at varying reading levels to further support the new learning by giving all students opportunities to be challenged through both problem-based and inquiry-based learning tasks
- Activities
  - brain-based vocabulary tasks to encourage students to stop at different times through the course of learning, think about the new vocabulary concepts (not just the definition, but all the connections to the word), and work at elaborating, reviewing, and meaning-making
  - cooperative learning groups using intentional, meaningful tasks to improve students' understanding of their standards-based content
  - Socratic seminars (a method of teaching developed by Socrates to engage students in intellectual discussion) following a specific

protocol to encourage students to think critically, analyze multiple meanings in text, and express ideas with clarity and confidence by reading assigned text and responding to open-ended questions within a group

o field trips, after first exposure to new content, in order to move from initial representational learning to concept learning

o Give One Get One activity (see Appendix B) to review the most recent learning

- Teaching strategies

o As students process content, provide them with immediate, meaningful, and appropriate feedback. Processing is a time of practice. It is a time for teachers to guide the students toward mastery. With that in mind, actual grades should be held at a minimum and used more during a summative assessment when the students are showing what they know and can do.

o Allow students to choose from a variety of activities through choice boards, independent learning assignments with contracts, and assigned learning workstations.

o Use moveable concept webs to process the relationships among ideas, theories, thoughts, and understandings within a unit of study.

o Vary the types of groups (partners, triads, small groups, and independent) in which students process new learning.

o Engage students in various management roles and dynamics with respect to other group members, and teach what that role looks and sounds like.

o Use questions at different levels of complexity.

o Use tiered assignments.

o Teach a variety of note-taking strategies and processing activities to make sense and meaning of those notes.

o Group students in ways that expose them to the perspectives of students of different races, genders, and cultures.

Technology- and Media-Related Approaches

Students who learn best through technology- and media-related approaches process content through various types of media. They are often given choices within criteria and guidelines set by the teacher. The learners may work independently, with partners, or in small groups.

- interactive media, such as Internet search engines, blogs, WebQuests on a variety of hardware, media exclusively used by the teacher or other students for presentations of new content

- music equipment
- virtual field trips created by teachers, other students, university websites, and commercial websites on topics that range from how food is supplied to the school cafeteria to a tour of the National Zoo with questions attached
- research using blogs and wikis for information to use in responding to reading or in critiquing movies
- writing, editing, and designing multimedia presentations, including slide shows using PowerPoint
- reflecting on and responding to open-ended questions about various live and on-demand audio and video streaming clips, which could include audio recordings of experts speaking about their fields of study or videos of a process in science
- use of text-to-speech software so that students can respond to the new content through their reflective writings, or search for additional content to extend or support their understanding
- use of WebQuests designed to add a new layer of understanding to initial processing

Strategies and Activities for Differentiating Student Products

Teachers differentiate student products (the projects, papers, presentations, or other physical outcomes that enable assessment of student learning) when they give students multiple opportunities to show what they know and can do with the new content and skills learned. A product is anything that results in showcasing a student's learning. In the past we might have considered only paper-pencil tests to be assessments. Those might have included multiple choice, fill-in-the-blank, true/false, or matching tests; diagrams to be labeled; or sometimes a request for a few sentences of written response.

In this current age of assessment, teachers are examining what students are learning on an ongoing basis, from the preassessment before a unit of study begins, through formative assessment to find out how instruction and grouping need to change, to the final products of tests, quizzes, written expressions, projects, demonstrations, and presentations. We continue to see much research and writing in this area, but many teachers still seem to be a bit nervous when it comes to using real-world products as authentic assessment pieces and valuing them as highly as they do written assignments.

Differentiating assessment should involve students in creating a portfolio of products throughout the course of a unit; these products highlight, in more than one way, what the students know and can do. For instance, a student who struggles to answer short-answer questions may be able to write an amazing response to open-ended high-level thinking questions. If the teacher only gave a multiple choice format of assessment, this student's portfolio would paint an incomplete picture of his or her actual understanding of the content. Some students are leaders when doing field study work and really show what they know in that context, but they are quieter during the Socratic seminar that is being used as a formative assessment. A variety of assessment experiences will give the teacher a truer picture of what each student knows.

An important part of this is that we as teachers must set high expectations for student work through the criteria we set for each assignment. Quite frankly, we don't have time for projects that are "cute" in a childlike way but don't show us much about what a student has learned. Work that students do is childlike anyway and amazing for that reason alone. But for assessments, we should expect them to do something of importance, something designed to achieve and demonstrate mastery of the content standard. In addition, each assignment should be engaging, respectful, and challenging. It should be valued, and if it is truly to be used as an assessment, it should "count" toward a student's grade just like paper-pencil quizzes or tests count. Some of the possibilities for differentiating products are listed below.

Concrete Approaches

These learners show what they know and can do through concrete approaches by using one or more of the five senses or through the multiple intelligences. Examples include the following:

- projects that allow students to use multiple intelligences and learning styles to represent their learning in concrete products, such as a brochure, sculpture, journal, model, dance, or flowchart
- lab experiments and field experiences scheduled after students learn and process given content to give them opportunities to solve project- or problem-based assessment tasks in a real-life setting
- variations in pacing based on students' accomplishments to make sense and meaning of content, giving them ample opportunities for practice and rehearsal

Representational Approaches

These learners show what they know and can do through a nonlinguistic approach, using few or no words. Examples of their work include drawing, role-playing, and the use of manipulatives. This approach is often accompanied by an explanation or presentation to a selective audience using identified criteria for both the product and the presentation.

- assignments that ask students to represent the new concepts developed over the course of a unit in paintings, illustrations, cartoons, diagrams, drawings, logos, or other nonlinguistic representations
- assignments that ask students to use charts, graphs, time lines, concept maps, or other visual representations to communicate information, for example, to show student-collected data, to show the results of research on a student-generated unit question, or other information to be shared

Abstract Approaches

These learners show what they know and can do by creating products and presentations that showcase their higher-level thinking skills, including observation, analysis, and evaluation.

- Use the "Ticket Into Class" protocol (see Appendix B) as a formative assessment: Individual students explain, either written or orally, what they understand after a particular chunk of learning so that the teacher knows how to progress in teaching and reteaching.
- Use cooperative learning groups and assessment tasks to assess and evaluate academic and behavioral goals. Each student within a cooperative group can first self-assess on his or her own, answering questions such as, Was I cooperative with time and materials? Did I use my time well and stay focused? Did I complete my required part of the task? Next, each student within the group assesses the group on their ability to work together: Did we cooperate with one another? Did we remain on task and finish the assignment appropriately? Did we keep everyone in the group safe? These questions can be more or less sophisticated based on the students' ages and grade level. Use a one to five rating level for older students, and a "yes" or "working on it" with the younger students.
- Use Socratic seminars (reading assigned text and responding to open-ended questions within a group) to formatively assess students' abilities to think critically, analyze multiple meanings in text, and express ideas with clarity and confidence. This will give you information to include in a summative assessment.
- Allow students to choose from among a variety of formative or summative tasks through choice boards; these tasks might include writing assignments or independent projects with a product and/or

presentation. Ask students questions about their products or presentations at different levels of complexity.

Technology- and Media-Related Approaches

These learners show what they know and can do by using a variety of media to fashion a product and presentation. The media are typically representative of what the teachers have used and taught within the classroom setting and may include blogs, WebQuests that are student designed, PowerPoint presentations of coinciding content, or music that relates to the content. The learners may work independently, with partners, or in small groups. They often have choice within criteria and guidelines set by the teacher.

- Blogs, wikis, and podcasts as products of research in the content areas
- Multimedia presentations including slide shows, video or audio productions, or WebQuests to showcase content and skills learned
- Reflection on and response to open-ended questions at varying levels of thinking—from comprehension and application to evaluation, analysis, and synthesis
- Use of text-to-speech software so that students can listen to quizzes and tests instead of reading them and respond to those test questions in a way that accurately shows their understanding of content and skills

DESIGN

Too often we give children answers to remember rather than problems to solve.

—Roger Lewin

Designing our tapestry requires knowing how to bring together the perfect threads and the delicate or sturdy or colorful fabrics to create the ideal design. That is true of differentiation also. In art there are many ways that thoughts, ideas, and life can be represented. In our classrooms, differentiation can be highlighted in many different ways, all of which are colorful, exciting, challenging, respectful, and dedicated to making students successful in the classroom. The success of differentiation depends on our intentional design of all the components within that framework.

Talking the Talk

Knowing how to implement the steps of differentiated instruction, as well as how and why to integrate it into a classroom, will give all teachers—both experienced and novice—a great plan for successful students. The guidelines that follow will help show the way, although you may choose to vary the steps to meet your specific needs.

How and When to Implement DI

Differentiation implies that teachers implement specific lessons designed intentionally for the students within their classes. Nothing is done by chance. Teachers know their students, know their content, know their standards, know how children learn, know good instruction, and then design lessons that are engaging, challenging, and supportive. The following are steps to implementing the DI philosophy in your school building:

1. **Develop PLCs.** In these groups, teachers engage in thoughtful work to improve their practice in specific ways in targeted areas over the course of a chosen time period. Topics might include evaluating student work, creating higher-order written response questions and tasks, building community within the school, learning to ask high-level questions of students, and finding and implementing great instructional strategies. PLCs are great ways to learn to observe students as you find colleagues who are ready to learn and grow. The protocol "Kid Watching" in Appendix B can help you with this.

2. **Review, evaluate, and implement national, state, and local standards.** Closely examine the content standards and district curriculum guides. Write out similar objectives into units. Create essential questions and a priority vocabulary web (a web that shows all of the vocabulary words and how they relate to one another) for each unit.

3. **Know your students.** In order to differentiate and meet your students' needs, you must know their strengths, interests, preferred learning styles, and areas of behavioral, social, and academic need. You can learn these through observations, learning profiles, conferences, interest inventories, preference surveys, and other formal and informal assessments.

4. **Create a positive classroom environment.** This includes addressing aspects of the environment such as the physical space, classroom management, flexible grouping, and the mood of the classroom. It includes working together with other classes at the same grade level

or content area on team projects, plays, and competitions. It involves using music, movement, humor, and praise. It means setting high standards and individual goals for all students. It means working with students to develop self-control and a lifelong passion for learning. School should be the most positive, safe place that our students go other than home. They should be able to take educational risks without the thought of embarrassment or humiliation. Students should know that as they are learning they have supportive teachers who will celebrate the small successes with them and help them advance toward their academic goals.

5. **Use preassessment tools.** Use several different, creative ways to preassess students in order to determine their levels of understanding and what should be taught to build upon what they already know. This preassessment can help initially in forming flexible groups of students who have similar skills. Based on pretest results and learning profiles, you will be ready to lay out a big picture of differentiation based on students' interests and readiness, the need-to-know in the curriculum, and resources available.

6. **Plan for intentional instruction.** Design content delivery, processing experiences, and assessment products intentionally so that students can show what they are learning and have learned over time. Examples include tiered assignments, curriculum compacting, higher-level thinking, learning centers, flexible groups, independent contracts, and choice boards.

7. **Integrate DI with RTI.** DI is at the heart of Tier 1 in the RTI framework. As preassessment and formative assessments identify students who continue to struggle with concepts and skills that other students are moving through successfully, design targeted interventions to help those students in Tier 2 gain positive momentum within the classroom.

8. **Complete summative assessments.** These final assessments determine whether students were able to meet given objectives at a high level. The standards determine what the goals are, but in using rubrics or scoring guides to show what the criteria for success should be and how the different levels of mastery look, teachers and students must have a clear understanding of the target. A rubric helps guide both you and your students in your quests for high achievement. When creating summative assessments, ask yourself, "Is this assessment *for* learning, or is this assessment *of* learning?" An assessment *for* learning is a cycle. It gives the student an opportunity to be

retaught, whether it's at the end of a chapter or at the end of the unit. The teacher disaggregates the data from the individual tests and self-assesses his or her own teaching to determine how the student could have learned more. Then, reteaching and reassessment begin for those students. Assessment *of* learning is an end in itself. Once a student is assessed, there is no reteaching on the part of the teacher. This is not to say that the student can't do independent study in some cases, but the school's teacher is generally out of the picture. The SAT is an example. Once the student has taken that test, the results are given, and we don't reteach or regive that assessment. Most generally, the state testing at the end of the year is an assessment *of* learning For instance, when we test our fifth graders, we may not get the results until the following year, and then different teachers usually have those students.

Differentiation is implemented in every class at a variety of entry points. Some teachers begin implementation with strategies and activities such as the following:

- Designing lessons with multiple ways to deliver content
- Intentionally stopping within the lesson to give students time to process the material
- Using formative assessments
- Using flexible grouping to have smaller groups for instruction
- Being intentional about classroom management strategies
- Using interest inventories and learning profiles to make learning relevant to students

Then teachers begin to move more intentionally into differentiation by adding to their repertoire of strategies, which might include some of the following:

- Using anchor activities, workstations, and centers to move all students forward academically while the teacher works with small groups
- Using preassessments to form initial flexible groups through interests or readiness to meet individual student needs
- Using additional formative assessments to guide instruction along the way
- Using a variety of summative assessments after chunks of learning and at the end of chapters and units of study
- Creating tiered activities

Finally, in addition to the above, full differentiation would include the following:

- Curriculum compacting and independent contracts for specific students
- Aligning curriculum with standards
- Designing the curriculum and its units with assessment first
- Keeping goals high for all students and addressing issues of fairness as they relate to grading in a differentiated classroom

Many parents and teachers alike believe that struggling students and special education students should be graded on a different scale than average and gifted students. In a standards-based classroom, students are graded against the standards. That is the measuring post. So everyone must get there. In that case, the rubric must be the same for everyone. What is different is the complexity of the assignments that are given to help students master the standard, or the amount of support that some students might receive in getting there, or the pacing for some students. But everyone is pushed and taught and retaught to get there. Some may barely make it to the edge of mastery, and others may go over the top, but the goal is for everyone to achieve mastery of the content standard.

Special education is supported by the reauthorization of the Individuals with Disabilities Education Act and has a federal mandate, and RTI is also supported by a federal mandate. DI is not required by any law, and yet it supports both RTI and special education. It is not regulated by any child's individualized education program (IEP), and it isn't written as an accommodation or modification. Differentiation is for all students in the classroom. Its purpose is to move students forward in their education by using the best student-centered instructional strategies that teachers can implement. It is giving students ownership in their learning and making multiple pathways for learning available for all students.

Differentiation may not be mandated, but it is an ethical and moral way to teach. When students don't understand new content, teachers have an obligation to reteach it in as many ways and as many times as it takes to get the students to a level of basic understanding. If we have students who continually fall behind, despite our bringing out a variety of differentiated strategies—from delivering content to experiences in processing, to changing their environments, to giving them more time— we can't let them languish. We must rely on our PLCs to collectively determine how, when, and where to introduce interventions. If what we are doing in the regular classroom with the differentiated strategies that we bring out to catch the students who seem to be falling behind doesn't make headway into what a particular student needs, then we move into interventions with RTI.

Appendix A has a "Differentiation of Instruction Walk Through Checklist" to assist you in the implementation of DI strategies, as well as a "Differentiation of Instruction Teacher Readiness Survey" to help teachers identify when they are ready for DI.

FRAME

Education is not filling a pail, but the lighting of a fire.

—William Butler Yeats

Nonnegotiables

Just as there are many ways to learn, there are also many ways to teach and differentiate instruction. But to succeed with DI, there are some aspects that are nonnegotiable. These are summarized in Table 3.2.

Table 3.2 What's In—What's Out

What's In	What's Out
• Student choice, time, and voice • Understanding the connections between PLCs, DI, and RTI • SMART goals for teachers and students that support DI (specific, measurable, actionable, realistic, time line) • Collecting data and using data in collegial conversations • Explicitly teaching and modeling the skills necessary to learn • Explicitly linking between instruction and assessment—formative and summative • Standards-based teaching • Understanding by design • Brain-based learning • Proactive interventions • Knowledge of student readiness and learning profiles	• Chaotic teaching • Tracking • Giving additional work to accelerated students • Watering down the curriculum • Test prep books • Meaningless themes or units • Teaching in a vacuum • Planning from the top down • Formative and summative assessments separate from instruction

REFERENCES AND RESOURCES

Allen, L. G., & Nickelsen, L. (2008). *Making words their own.* Peterborough, NH: Crystal Springs Books.

Allington, R. L. (1983). The reading instruction provided readers of differing abilities. *The Elementary School Journal, 83,* 548–559.

Bailey, B. (2001). *Conscious discipline* (Rev. ed.). Oviedo, FL: Loving Guidance.

Blackburn, B. (2008). *Rigor is not a four-letter word.* Larchmont, NY: Eye on Education.

Brookfield, S. (2006). *The skillful teacher. On technique, trust, and responsiveness in the classroom.* San Francisco, CA: Jossey-Bass.

Campbell, B. (2007). *Using multiple intelligences to differentiate instruction.* New York: Allyn & Bacon.

Center for Implementing Technology in Education, Research Center. (n.d.). *Learning mathematics with virtual manipulatives.* Retrieved from http://www.cited.org/index.aspx?page_id=151

Create a Graph. http://nces.ed.gov/nceskids/createagraph/default.aspx

Diller, D. (2008). *Spaces and places: designing classrooms for literacy.* Portland, ME: Stenhouse.

Dreeben, R., & Barr, R. (1988). The formation and instruction of ability groups. *American Journal of Education, 97,* 34–61.

Forsten, C., Goodman, G., Grant, J., Hollas, B., & Whyte, D. (2006). *The more ways you teach the more students you reach.* Peterborough, NH: Crystal Springs Books.

Fountas, I., & Pinnell, G. S. (1996). *Guided reading: Good first teaching for all children.* Portsmouth, NH: Heinemann.

Fountas, I., & Pinnell, G. S. (2001). *Guiding readers and writers: Teaching comprehension, genre, and content literacy.* Portsmouth, NH: Heinemann.

Goodman, Y. M., & Goodman, K. S. (1990). Vygotsky in a whole language perspective. In L. Moll (Ed.), *Vygotsky and education* (pp. 223–250). London, UK: Cambridge University Press.

Gregory, G., & Chapman, C. (2002). *Differentiated instruction strategies: One size doesn't fit all.* Thousand Oaks, CA: Corwin.

Jensen, E. (2003). *Tools of engagement: Managing learner states for learner success.* San Diego, CA: The Brain Store.

Jensen, E. (2005). *Teaching with the brain in mind* (2nd ed.). Alexandria, VA: Association for Supervision and Curriculum Development.

Jensen, E., & Nickelsen, L. (2008). *Deeper learning.* Thousand Oaks, CA: Corwin.

Marzano, R. J. (2001). *Classroom instruction that works: Research-based strategies for increasing student achievement.* Alexandria, VA: Association for Supervision and Curriculum Development.

Marzano, R. J. (2003). *What works in schools: Translating research into action.* Alexandria, VA: Association for Supervision and Curriculum Development.

National Library of Virtual Manipulatives. http://nlvm.usu.edu/en/nav/vlibrary.html

Partnership for 21st Century Skills. (2004). *Framework for 21st century learning.* Retrieved from http://www.p21.org/index.php?option=com_content&task=view&id=254&Itemid=119

Peterson, R. (1992). *Life in a crowded place: Making a learning community.* Portsmouth, NH: Heinemann.

Smith, R. (2004). *Conscious classroom management: Unlocking the secrets of great teaching.* San Rafael, CA: Conscious Teaching.

Sousa, D. A. (2001). *How the brain learns* (2nd ed.) Thousand Oaks, CA: Corwin.

Sousa, D. A. (2006). *How the brain learns* (3rd ed.). Thousand Oaks, CA: Corwin.

Tomlinson, C. A. (1999). *The differentiated classroom: Responding to the needs of all learners.* Alexandria, VA: Association for Supervision and Curriculum Development.

Tomlinson, C. A. (2001). *How to differentiate instruction in mixed-ability classrooms.* Alexandria, VA: Association for Supervision and Curriculum Development.

Tomlinson, C. A. (2003). *Fulfilling the promise of the differentiated classroom.* Alexandria, VA: Association for Supervision and Curriculum Development.

VanderWeide, D. (2005). *Different tools for different learners.* New York: Scholastic.

Weaver, C. (1988). *Reading process and practice: From socio-psycholinguistics to whole language.* Portsmouth, NH: Heinemann.

WebQuest. http://www.webquest.org

Wolfe, P. (2001). *Brain matters: Translating research into classroom practice.* Alexandria, VA: Association for Supervision and Curriculum Development.

Wormeli, R. (2006). *Fair isn't always equal: Assessing and grading in the differentiated classroom.* Portland, ME: Stenhouse.

Wormeli, R. (2007). *Differentiation: From planning to practice, grades 6–12.* Portland, ME: Stenhouse.

4 Response to Intervention

THREADS

When we cast our bread upon the waters we can presume that someone downstream whose face we may never see will benefit from our action, even as we enjoy the gifts sent to us from a donor upstream.

—Maya Angelou

What It Is

Response to Intervention (RTI) is a general education initiative that was written into the Individuals with Disabilities Education Act in 2004 to offer educators a framework in which to structure early intervening services and meet the needs of all students. Through RTI, schools can determine what is working, what is not, and what to do about it.

RTI offers a system for planning, instruction, assessment, and intervention that helps schools identify and help struggling students earlier than they would normally get help in a teaching situation. Through appropriate instruction and interventions, educators can increase the likelihood that more students will be successful. As a result, special education is no longer a "dumping ground" for those students teachers are unsure how to handle or teach.

RTI targets both behavior and academic achievement. Most educators recognize that these two areas are inextricably connected and that high expectations in one area directly impact student progress in the other. Studies have actually shown that when schools raised their behavioral expectations of students, the students' academic achievement improved, and vice versa (Hawkins, Catalano, Kosterman, Abbott, & Hill, 1999).

The RTI model is multitiered, usually with three tiers, but sometimes with more or fewer. Tier 1 is the general education classroom. Within the RTI framework, it is expected that 80% to 85% of the students will be successful in this tier. The use of evidence-based core instruction is essential here, as the teacher's goal is to help as many students as possible be successful and maintain class placement. Differentiated instruction is crucial in planning, instruction, and assessment in Tier 1. It is in the general education classroom where universal screening occurs—usually three times per year at the earlier grades, and fewer times for students in the upper grades. Instruction is typically focused on the whole classroom or small groups within it.

Typically, 10% to 15% of the students in the general education classroom have difficulty in reading or math. Within the RTI framework, these students who are at risk receive short-term, targeted interventions designed to help them overcome their deficits and decrease the achievement gap. These students are monitored regularly to determine their progress or lack thereof. Tier 2 targeted interventions are usually focused on small groups or individuals.

The students who show no progress after Tier 2 interventions receive Tier 3 intensive interventions. Usually 5% to 10% of the students require these frequent interventions to meet their individual learning needs. In some states and districts, Tier 3 is equivalent to special education. More typically, it is the final tier before referral to special education, which may be considered Tier 4.

Two Models

There are two models of RTI—the Problem-Solving Model and the Standard Protocol Model. As you read about the features of each in Table 4.1, you will notice that the differences between the two models occur in Tier 2. Although some schools have elected to use one model or the other, many have determined that a combination of the two models seems to work best.

Table 4.1 Two Models of RTI

	Problem-Solving Model	**Standard Protocol Model**
Tier 1	All students receive universal screening and high-quality, evidence-based instruction. Progress is monitored traditionally (anecdotal notes, observation notations, etc.).	

	Problem-Solving Model	Standard Protocol Model
Tier 2	Students whose Tier 1 progress is not adequate receive additional support. 1. Teaching team makes instructional decisions based on each student's performance. 2. Individual students receive a variety of evidence-based interventions. 3. Interventions are individualized for each student. Progress is monitored weekly through the use of curriculum-based measurement tools, etc.	Students whose Tier 1 progress is not adequate receive additional support. 1. Person delivering intervention makes instructional decisions following standard protocol. 2. Small groups of students with similar needs are presented with standard, evidence-based interventions. 3. Intervention is delivered in a predetermined format to allow for greater quality control. Progress is monitored weekly through the use of curriculum-based measurement tools, etc.
Tier 3	Students whose Tier 2 progress is inadequate may receive more intensive intervention. Depending on the state, these students may qualify either for special education services or learning disability evaluation. Progress is monitored frequently, based upon student need.	

Source: Adapted from The IRIS Center (2007).

The Research Behind It

As the connecting thread within our integrated tapestry, research on the effects of early intervention has been a driving force for the development and implementation of RTI. Before RTI, the federal government recognized IQ-achievement discrepancy as the primary operational definition of a learning disability (LD) (U.S. Office of Education, 1977). This IQ discrepancy model identified a learning disability as based on a severe discrepancy between a student's intelligence and his or her achievement test scores. This meant that a student had to show a great difference between what the average student at that age and IQ should be able to know and do and what that student actually did know and could do (such as a specific learning disability or mental retardation) to qualify for specialized instruction or interventions. Often described as "waiting to fail," this approach frequently resulted in delaying intervention until students had fallen so far behind that they could not catch up. In addition, the number of students identified as having an LD increased dramatically, resulting in burgeoning special education enrollment and costs (Fuchs & Fuchs, 2006; Fuchs, Mock, Morgan, & Young, 2003).

Whereas the IQ model focused on identifying student deficits and reacting to them, RTI provides a framework for LD identification and the design of early instruction and intervention that is proactive in nature. There is a definite connection between identification of disabilities and instruction to correct them (Vaughn & Fuchs, 2003). RTI focuses on providing early and immediate support for struggling students by screening all students as early as kindergarten (Fletcher, Coulter, Reschly, & Vaughn 2004; Vaughn & Fuchs, 2003). The effectiveness of this type of early intervention has been and continues to be supported by a variety of studies, including the following:

- The National Summit on Learning Disabilities (2001)
- The President's Commission on Excellence in Special Education (2002)
- The National Research Center on Learning Disabilities Common Ground Report (2002)
- The National Institute for Child Health and Development (ongoing)

Who Said It and Why

RTI has been endorsed by many researchers and organizations (Fletcher et al., 2004; Fuchs et al., 2003). In their research on ways to predict success in early literacy intervention, Leslie and Allen (1999) documented the effectiveness of early intervention to prevent later difficulties.

In reviewing some of the applications targeted through the RTI framework, Mellard and Johnson (2008) determined the following:

- Screening and prevention
  - o identifies students who are at risk.
  - o provides early intervention.
- Early intervention
  - o enhances the general curriculum for all students.
  - o provides intervention and remediation.
- Disability determination
  - o determines a student's response to instruction.
  - o determines a student's response to intervention.

In her article titled "No More 'Waiting to Fail': How Response to Intervention Works and Why It Is Needed," Brown-Chidsey (2007) points out that RTI provides equal education opportunities for all students.

Through the RTI framework, students can receive instruction and interventions without the "stigmatizing effects of a disability label." Other research included in this article includes the following:

- RTI raises education attainment of students in general and reduces the number of students who need special education (Brown-Chidsey & Steege, 2005).
- The earlier the intervention, the better the outcomes for students identified as being at risk for reading problems (Speece, Case, & Molloy, 2003).
- RTI methods used over time reduce total special education placements and improve academic outcomes for students at risk (O'Connor, 2003; Tilly, 2003).

ESSENCE

The formulation of the problem is often more important than the solution.

—Albert Einstein

Since RTI is a federally mandated initiative, educators do not have a choice about whether or not they will implement it. However, in order to be successful, educators must make informed choices about *what* aspects of RTI work best for their student population, *why* RTI has the potential for being a good thing, and *how* RTI directly impacts their own teaching and their students' learning. Appendix A includes a form, "Response to Intervention Teacher Readiness Survey," that will help determine your school's readiness to implement RTI.

What's in It for Me?

When looking at any kind of change, educators are often cautious about welcoming it with open arms. Based on prior experience, they suspect there will be extra work that may include attending more meetings, filling out more paperwork, being expected to learn and implement new strategies, and not having follow-up support. A common question is "What's in it for me?" In the case of RTI, four answers that address this question follow.

- **Support system.** An essential element of RTI is collaboration. Instead of working in isolation, teachers work as team members with each other and with their administrators in defining specific learning or behavior problems, planning and implementing interventions, and evaluating student progress. Unlike the old model of education, where teachers literally or figuratively closed their doors and made all of their own decisions, they do not have to do everything alone.

- **Sense of efficacy.** Through collegial conversations and sharing, teachers focus on each other's strengths and the knowledge each brings to the table. As they learn to trust each other, it becomes easier to share not only what is working but also what is not. As they learn to offer and accept help, they discover that each person is a valuable asset to the team.

- **Students more engaged, motivated, and successful.** Every teacher dreams about having a classroom where students want to be, are actively involved in the learning, and are making appropriate progress. When implemented with fidelity, the key components of RTI make those outcomes more likely. With its focus on early identification of learning or behavior issues, differentiated instruction at Tier 1, and differentiated interventions in Tiers 2 and 3, RTI allows educators to be proactive rather than reactive in the ways they teach and relate to students.

- **Focus on what students need academically and behaviorally.** Most teachers have a passion for teaching and kids. They certainly didn't go into teaching to make money! They want to do what is best for their students. As is the case with differentiated instruction, in the RTI framework the focus is *not* on a one-size-fits-all program. Instead, teachers work with their colleagues to plan, implement, and assess the instruction and interventions each student needs. Making learning relevant to each student creates that environment for motivation and success.

21st Century Skills

In the RTI framework, focusing on our students' needs means we must stop and consider who they are now as well as what they must know and be able to do as they become adults. In its Framework for 21st Century Learning, the Partnership for 21st Century Skills (n.d.) identified the following skills as being necessary for success:

- Critical thinking and problem solving
- Creativity and innovation
- Communication and collaboration

As our student population becomes more and more diverse, and as technology continues to change exponentially, we must explore ways to differentiate content, process, and product to promote problem-solving and decision-making skills in each tier. All students should learn to self-assess their own progress and growth in order to become independent and self-motivated learners. They must learn the skills that allow them to think and communicate, work in teams, have self-control, think flexibly, and be persistent. Understanding students' learning styles, modalities, and multiple intelligences can guide teachers in providing appropriate choices for learning and demonstrating mastery of content standards and skills, but understanding a student's learning profile also helps teachers mentor a student in the "habits of mind" (Costa & Kallick, 2000) that are needed to sustain learning. Figure 4.1 provides a summary of the different intelligences to help teachers select learning activities.

Figure 4.1 Multiple Intelligences

Visual/Spatial

As the mind conceptualizes ideas about its surrounding environment, it often employs the visual/spatial intelligence of images, pictures, and graphical representations.

Logical/Mathematical

This intelligence encompasses an entire range of reasoning skills. From the logic of Sherlock Holmes to the wisdom of Winston Churchill, the logical/mathematical intelligence charts the data, information, and facts in the human mind.

Verbal/Linguistic

The power of the word, in its myriad forms, is truly at the heart of this intelligence. Reading, writing, and other forms of communication, such as sign language, also reside under this umbrella.

Musical/Rhythmic

The power of music cannot be overlooked as a primary channel for learning and knowing, sharing and expressing, and perceiving and creating pitch and patterns for the human mind.

Bodily/Kinesthetic

Action is the key to this intelligence. The body is the conduit for the mind, and muscle memory obtained from experiences is what defines the bodily/kinesthetic intelligence.

Interpersonal/Social

This intelligence stems from people's interactions. Embodied in this intelligence are the give-and-take of communication and an understanding of others and their motivations as well as an ability to effectively empathize with their feelings.

(Continued)

Figure 4.1 (Continued)

Intrapersonal/Introspective

This intelligence carries the message, "Know thyself." It represents a frame of mind in which learners internalize learning through thoughtful connections and then transfer it to novel situations through reflective application.

Naturalist

The naturalist intelligence discovers subtle change in the environment. It collects, sorts, and categorizes articles and objects from the natural world, and it organizes those collections by classifying, labeling, and keeping notebooks.

Existentialist

Gardner describes this intelligence as "the intelligence of big questions." The existentialist seeks answers to fundamental questions of being, such as Where do we come from? What happens when we die? Why does war exist?

Source: Adapted from Fogarty & Stoehr (2008).

Making It Rigorous

In her book, *Rigor Is Not a Four-Letter Word* (2008), Barbara Blackburn defines rigor as "creating an environment in which each student is expected to learn at high levels, each student is supported so he or she can learn at high levels, and each student demonstrates learning at high levels" (p. 16). She describes four characteristics of expecting students to learn at high levels:

- high expectations
- a challenging curriculum
- instruction that includes high-level questioning
- instruction that includes differentiation and multiple intelligences

In the RTI framework, all students are supported and challenged so they can learn at their highest levels. As with differentiated instruction, everyone is expected not only to learn the content required by the standards but also to demonstrate mastery of it. The curriculum is based on local, state, and/or national standards. Teacher teams should revisit their standards every year in order to prioritize them by looking for those standards that carry more weight and, consequently, should receive more instructional time.

As schools implement RTI, they must consider how to best incorporate evidence-based core instruction at Tier 1 and evidence-based interventions at Tiers 2 and 3. Bloom's Taxonomy of Educational Objectives, now revised as the New Bloom's Taxonomy, provides an excellent framework for helping teachers move developing learners from concrete, lower-level thinking to more complex, higher-level thinking. Through differentiated strategies, such as cubing and tiering, all learners can be challenged at their appropriate levels of thinking.

As Blackburn (2008) suggests, high-level questioning is another way to create a rigorous learning environment. The questions we teachers ask frame the thought processes of our students. Our goal in every tier must be to get *all* learners to think, process, and respond at higher levels. If high-level questioning is new to you, consider starting simply by identifying your questions as either "fat" or "skinny." Fat questions are usually open ended, take time to think through and answer, and often require discussion and explanation. Fat questions typically begin with "What if . . . ? "Why . . . ?" and "How . . . ?" Skinny questions generally require simple, one-word or one-phrase answers and take very little time or thought. They often begin with "Who . . . ?" "What . . . ?" "When . . . ?" or "Where . . . ?" (Fogarty & Stoehr, 2008). Table 4.2 summarizes the difference between the two.

Table 4.2 Fat and Skinny Questions

"Fat" Question Stems	"Skinny" Question Stems
Why . . . ? How . . . ? What if . . . ?	Who . . . ? What . . . ? When . . . ? Where . . . ?

Blackburn (2008) recommends differentiated instruction and targeting the multiple intelligences as ways to guide students to higher-level learning. Within the RTI framework, planning for differentiated instruction and interventions is essential in making learning rigorous for all students in every tier.

As you work to make your classroom more rigorous, consider what rigor is *not:*

- More homework
- For your advanced students only
- Punishment

FABRIC

Good teaching is not magic, and it is not based solely on intuition.

—Eric Jensen

Like professional learning communities (PLCs) and differentiated instruction (DI), RTI has a specific purpose and is a staple in the 21st century classroom. Teaching is flexible rather than rigid in order to meet students where they are, not where we think they should be. Learning is natural rather than contrived, focusing on life skills and content standards. And planning is collaborative rather than isolated, strengthening the entire fabric of the RTI framework.

Walking the Walk

Whether you are implementing PLCs, DI, or RTI, fidelity is essential to the overall success and accountability of the initiative. All components, as well as instruction and interventions, must be delivered with integrity and authenticity in the way they were designed, tested, and evaluated by the authors. That is the only way you will be able to accurately determine if a student's performance is genuine.

When implemented with fidelity, RTI has the potential to

- decrease the achievement gap,
- increase student success,
- increase student independence and learning,
- lower the dropout rate, and
- keep special education from becoming a dumping ground.

Defining Components

Chapter 3 presented a variety of ways to differentiate content, process, and product through concrete, representational, abstract, and technology- and media-related approaches. These approaches are essential in the RTI framework as well, and they should be woven into each of these key components of RTI:

1. Comprehensive universal screening

2. Progress monitoring

3. Evidence-based core instruction

4. Data-based decision making

5. Evidence-based interventions

Comprehensive Universal Screening

The purpose of universal screening is to identify students who may be at risk in reading or math. While it may not identify specific problems, the screening indicates areas (such as comprehension, vocabulary, computation, problem solving, etc.) in which a student may potentially struggle. Using the data from universal screening, teachers can compare group and individual performance on specific skills and then differentiate instruction appropriately. These data can also provide evidence of the effectiveness of the core curriculum and instruction. For instance, if the results indicate that a large percentage of students are struggling in a specific area, it is likely that a gap exists, either in *what* is being taught or in the *way* in which it is being taught.

Universal screening

- should be quick and cost-effective or free.
- occurs during general instruction in Tier 1.
- has a role in predicting future performance.
- is usually conducted three times over the school year in early grades and once or twice yearly thereafter; individual school districts make this decision. Screening instruments can be web based but can also be created by educators in the school district.

Progress Monitoring

Progress monitoring includes a variety of short assessments that result in usable data. These data guide the development of instructional strategies and the use of appropriate curriculum to address areas in which students are struggling. Progress monitoring provides information and documentation that can be used to guide student placement decisions. Student performance determines whether instructional modifications and interventions are necessary.

Progress monitoring

- focuses on accurately representing students' current learning and performance.
- is administered repeatedly and over short periods of time.
- should be used in Tier 1 as needed, based on student progress; in Tier 2 two times per week or more; and in Tier 3 three times per week to daily.

- can be used to determine both performance and growth in the relevant skill.
- may be web based, or educators may create their own.

Evidence-Based Core Instruction

Evidence-based core instruction occurs at Tier 1, which is the general education classroom level. High-quality evidence-based instruction has been proven to be effective for most students (Batsche et al., 2005). In many instances, the use of appropriate instructional strategies by the classroom teacher determines whether or not a student can maintain class placement. There are numerous excellent resources for evidence-based instruction. Appendix C includes a sampling of those resources.

Data-Based Decision Making

The data we receive from universal screening, progress monitoring, and other types of assessments should inform our instructional decisions in every tier. It should help us identify students who are at risk and guide our design of targeted and intensive interventions for those struggling learners. It should also provide a means for evaluating the effectiveness of the existing curriculum and instruction. Data can be collected formally or informally, as the list below indicates.

- Formal assessments
  - Standardized tests
  - Textbook exams
  - Curriculum-based measurements
  - Universal screening
  - Progress monitoring
- Informal assessments
  - Observations
  - Quick quiz or Ticket Into Class (see Appendix B)
  - Journals
  - Surveys
  - Writing samples, such as those from student conferencing and goal setting
  - Other student work

Within the RTI framework, data and documentation go hand in hand. In order to be valid, the data must be recorded. *To be legal, unless it is documented, it did not happen.* There are many ways to record data. Anecdotal

Notes is a simple but effective tool when observing students in Tier 2 or 3. Table 4.3 is an example of Anecdotal Notes; it displays data collected on a struggling student named Greyson.

Table 4.3 Anecdotal Notes

Student _____

Date	Observation Notes	Next Steps
9/15	• Brainstorming topic ideas for persuasive essay. • Having difficulty selecting and focusing on just one topic.	• Peer conference to help her narrow her topics down to two. • Remind her how to create and use RAFT (role, audience, format, topic) strategy demonstrated in class. • Help her create a RAFT to focus her on a topic.
9/17	• Working on organization and content of essay. Struggling with sequence and summarization.	• Show her how to develop her essay using an advanced organizer (4 Square). Help her determine and place lead sentences for each paragraph in appropriate box of organizer.
9/19	• Transferring sentences from advanced organizer to notebook. • Adding sentences to each paragraph.	• Begin editing after writing and rereading her essay.

Evidence-Based Interventions

Evidence-based interventions target learning or behavior problems through specific strategies that are different from those that occur in the general education classroom. They rely on measurements that provide valid data and use systematic, explicit methods to change performance or behavior, such as the Gradual Release of Responsibility model. In this model, the teacher first *models* a specific strategy. Then the strategy is *shared* with the learners as the teacher offers direction and support. Third, the strategy is *guided* when the teacher expects students to use the strategy in small group settings. During this step, the teacher steps back and monitors students' use of the strategy. And finally, each student is expected to use the strategy *independently*. The teacher monitors the students both directly and indirectly by observing them and by reviewing their work.

When used correctly, this model is an effective way to move from teacher-directed to student-directed learning and ownership.

Gradual Release of Responsibility Model

Modeled ——————▶ Shared ——————▶ Guided ——————▶ Independent

In an effort to better understand what evidence-based interventions are, it may be helpful to identify what they are not.

Evidence-based interventions are *not* the following:

- Classroom observations
- Retention
- Suspension
- Shortened assignments
- Changing seating
- Parent conferences
- Making up homework

Following is a brief description of interventions that may occur in each tier. Keep in mind that the amount of time in an intervention should be proportional to the extent the student is behind. If three to five sets of data from the progress monitoring instrument indicate that a student is displaying growth due to an intervention, the teacher and team members will need to decide whether to keep the student where he or she is, or move him or her to a different tier.

Tier 1 Intervention

- Has a goal of helping all students achieve grade-level performance benchmarks in the general education classroom
- Should include explicit and systematic modeling and practice linking prior knowledge to new content and skills
- Has a duration based on student needs and weight or complexity of content standard
- Typically is part of comprehensive literacy or math curriculum

Tier 2 Intervention

- Is *targeted* to support a student's particular area of need
- Generally has a duration of six to nine weeks with regular progress monitoring, documenting, and conferring

- Typically is provided three to four times a week, with the length of each session commensurate with the student's age and degree of need
- Is conducted by trained and/or supervised personnel

Tier 3 Intervention

- Is *intensive* to support a student's particular area of need
- Generally has a duration of nine to twelve weeks with regular progress monitoring, documenting, and conferring
- Typically is provided every other day or daily, with session length commensurate with student's age and degree of need
- Is conducted by highly trained and/or supervised personnel

DESIGN

In times of great change, it's not unusual to miss the obvious.

—Stephen Wilmarth

Now that we have explored the thread, essence, and fabric of RTI, it is time to narrow the focus to its design. How can we make implementation less complicated and more achievable? What kind of time line should we follow? Who should be involved in the stages of implementation? How can we weave RTI, PLC, and DI together in an integrated tapestry?

Talking the Talk

As you implement RTI in your school, think about ways it can interface with your existing structures and curricula. In other words, don't throw the baby out with the bath water. Analyze your daily schedule and available space to determine if there are issues that will impact interventions. Some schools have actually inserted a 30-minute "intervention period" into each day by making adjustments to other parts of the schedule. In many general education classrooms, teachers are conducting Tier 2 interventions during flexible grouping. Also, think about the personnel you already have. Determine if or how certain individuals' roles may need to change in order to meet the requirements of RTI.

In order for RTI to be successful, your school must have a collaborative and participative culture. All stakeholders—that is, anyone directly or indirectly affected—should be involved in discussions about fidelity of implementation—what it means, what it looks like in the RTI framework, and how teachers are to be accountable. Make sure everyone understands that the purpose of RTI is *not* to blame teachers for poor student results but rather to support teachers in their efforts to help all students become successful. Another discussion should focus on decision rules within the RTI framework. These rules provide the guidelines for determining when an intervention should be changed, when a student should be moved from one tier to another, and when a student may be considered for special education.

How and When to Implement RTI

Remember that early intervention is essential. At the elementary level, this should mean

- *not* waiting for the psychologist to test a student.
- *not* waiting for the student to fall far enough behind to be considered a failure.
- *not* waiting for the correct discrepancy to surface.
- *not* waiting until third grade to provide services.

At *all* levels, early intervention means diagnosing those struggling students early in the school year and providing differentiated instruction and interventions to support their learning and/or behavior needs. It means using the data we receive from assessments such as screening and progress monitoring to make instructional adjustments sooner rather than later. And it means determining whether you will make those data-based decisions on your own (Standard Protocol Model), as part of a problem-solving team (Problem-Solving Model), or in a way that combines both, as described earlier in this chapter.

Time Line for Implementation

Typically, RTI is implemented over a period of one to three years, depending upon other initiatives that are already in place. For instance, if a PLC is established in your school, that forms the framework for your RTI collaborative discussions. Likewise, if the teachers are routinely differentiating instruction at Tier 1, they are already implementing one of the key components of RTI, which is evidence-based core instruction. More important than the number of years needed to implement RTI are the phases through which your school will progress. Some phases will take longer than others, and some will occur concurrently. Table 4.4 organizes RTI implementation into three phases.

Table 4.4	Time Line for RTI Implementation
Phase 1	• Establish a Professional Learning Community. • Differentiate instruction in Tier 1. • Conduct professional development on RTI. • Begin an Action Plan (see below). • Set up RTI teams. • Select an RTI model. • Choose or design a method for universal screening and begin using it.
Phase 2	• Hold discussions on decision rules, fidelity of implementation, and documentation procedures. • In Tier 1, regularly use data from assessments to make instructional decisions. • Make decisions about when and how interventions for Tiers 2 and 3 will be conducted. • Choose or design a method for progress monitoring and begin using it. • Begin differentiating interventions in Tiers 2 and 3. • Finish Action Plan.
Phase 3	• In all tiers, use data to make most instruction and intervention decisions. • Differentiate instruction and interventions consistently. • Evaluate practicality and usefulness of universal screening and progress monitoring.

Action Plan

An important part of implementing RTI or any other initiative is creating and following an action plan. It is designed around questions such as, What are our goals? What should we do first? What specific steps must we take to accomplish our goals? What is our time line? Appendix A includes a sample Action Plan that reflects the use of SMART goals; that is, goals that are specific, measurable, actionable, and realistic and that have a reasonable time line. It also includes a Work Plan template to help you plan your improvement effort and support implementation.

Why We Should Integrate It

With Professional Learning Communities. PLCs provide the vehicle through which collaborative discussions can take place. As educators develop trusting relationships with their colleagues, they can have honest conversations around questions such as the following:

- What do we want our students to learn?
- How will we know when each student has mastered the content standards?
- What do we do when a student does not learn?
- What do we do when a student already knows the content we're teaching?

Members of RTI teams or instructional support teams are often on other teams, as well. In their vertical or departmental teams, they prioritize or "unpack" content standards, identify resources to determine depth and rigor of the standards, analyze curricula, and discuss what students should know and be able to do at each grade level. In their horizontal or cross-curricular teams, teachers discuss ways to integrate curricula as well as how to better meet the academic and behavioral needs of students within their grade levels or communities. The information from both of these teams is invaluable in designing instruction and interventions within the RTI framework.

Building relationships is vital to the success of RTI, since it sometimes really does take a village to help one child succeed. Through PLCs, those relationships are fostered among colleagues, with family members, with community businesses, and with agencies and organizations. Everyone associated with the school should be a part of building relationships—administrators, teachers, paraprofessionals, coaches, resource personnel, consultants, nurses, counselors and psychologists, secretaries, custodians, cooks and cafeteria workers, guards, and bus drivers. And they should understand that their roles may be critical if they are included in an RTI team for a student's academic or behavior needs.

With Differentiated Instruction. For RTI to succeed, the core instruction in Tier 1 must be responsive, driven by data, and standards based. In the differentiated classroom, the teacher plans for and responds to students' needs through concrete, representational, abstract, and technology- and media-related strategies. Instruction and grouping are determined by data from a variety of assessments. And content, process, and product are differentiated around the local, state, and national content standards. Because all students think and learn differently, it makes sense that the interventions at Tiers 2 and 3 should be differentiated, as well.

One of the goals of RTI is to support students who are at risk by removing barriers to learning. In differentiated classrooms, teachers find out how individual students learn best and what interests them, and identify any other information that might impact their academic performance and behavior. They then differentiate instruction using this information. For instance, a student who is highly tactile-kinesthetic will be given opportunities to learn and process new information through hands-on experiences, such as going on field trips, using manipulatives, or conducting experiments.

Another goal of RTI is to help schools work more efficiently and effectively in addressing the needs of all learners. In the differentiated classroom, teachers make instructional decisions based on data, not hunches. They use preassessments, formative assessments, and summative assessments to collect and analyze data, and then they address student progress and growth (or lack thereof). In addition, they use classroom time flexibly in order to meet the needs of all learners.

How to Integrate It

With Professional Learning Communities. One of the first steps on the time line for RTI implementation is to create an RTI team or instructional support team. Figure 4.2 lists possible team members; membership will vary depending on the student's specific issues. Leadership on the team changes depending on the situation, that is, whether the issues are academic, behavioral, emotional, or a combination.

Figure 4.2 Possible RTI Team Members

Team may include all or some of the following, depending on student/situation.	
• Classroom teacher(s) • Special education teacher • Title I or ELL staff • Administrator • Coach (literacy, math, etc.) • Speech pathologist • Family member(s)	• Counselor • Psychologist • Nurse • Support staff • Social worker • Community agencies • Other school employees

Earlier in this chapter, it was suggested that collaborative discussions occur around RTI issues such as program fidelity and decision rules. Throughout these discussions, educators should also talk about product and program quality, student and teacher expectations, and grading. The questions presented in Figure 4.3 are designed to jump-start further conversations within the RTI framework.

In the DPIE Problem-Solving Model presented by Bender and Shores (2007), team members first *define* the problem using data from universal

Figure 4.3 Collaborative Discussions

Classroom Instruction

- What does the curriculum look like?
- Are there any redundancies or gaps in the curriculum?
- What content standards need more instructional time? What strategies are we using?

Struggling Students

- What data do we have?
- How are we using the data?
- How are we differentiating for students who are not making enough progress?
- What interventions are we using?

General Student Concerns

- What data do we have?
- What additional data do we need?
- What are the data telling us?
- Are we progress-monitoring the right students?

Strategies to Share

- What is working?
- What is not working?
- What additional support do we need?
- How can we improve the process?

screening, progress monitoring, and other forms of assessment. Next, they *plan* an intervention, determining who will conduct it, how long it will last, and how many times it will be given. The intervention is then *implemented* according to the plan. And finally, the student's progress is *evaluated*. As is evident in Figure 4.4, the process is cyclical. If the student does not progress as expected, the team goes back to the drawing board to redefine the problem, plan and implement a new intervention, and once again evaluates the student's performance.

With Differentiated Instruction. In the integrated tapestry, differentiation drives *instruction* at Tier 1, *targeted* interventions at Tier 2, and *intensive* interventions at Tier 3, as shown in Figure 4.5.

In Tier 1, the teacher gathers data through a variety of assessments in order to differentiate content delivery, student processing, and demonstration of mastery. In the differentiated classroom, the teacher is a diagnostician, constantly assessing and documenting student academic performance and behavior. Preassessments give the teacher an overall picture of where the students are in their understanding of a topic, unit, or concept. They

Figure 4.4 Problem-Solving Model (DPIE)

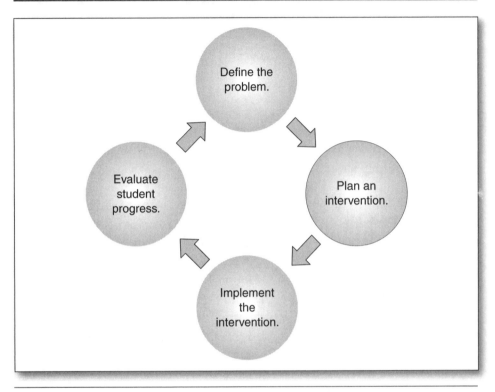

Source: Bender & Shores (2007).

Figure 4.5 Integrating RTI and DI

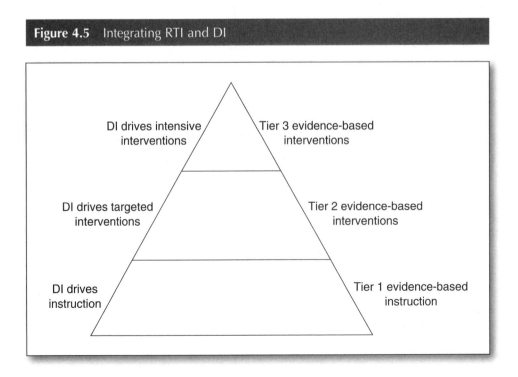

answer the questions, "What do my students know?" and "What are my students able to do?" Formative assessments answer the question, "What are my students learning?" at specific times during a course of study. At the end of a unit of study, summative assessments answer the question, "What have my students learned and at what depths?"

"ABC Brainstorm" is a favorite preassessment among teachers of grades 4–12. Sometimes called "ABC Graffiti," this assessment focuses on vocabulary and activates prior knowledge about a topic. It can also be used as a formative assessment to determine whether students' vocabularies are developing as the unit of study progresses.

Working either individually or with partners, students brainstorm words that relate to the topic given to them by the teacher. The topic is a direct connection to the upcoming unit. Using a form that lists all the letters of the alphabet (see Appendix A for a reproducible copy), students work for approximately two minutes to write words that relate to the upcoming unit. For example, in a unit on weather, a student might write *clouds* on the C line, *thunder* on the T line, and *barometer* on the B line. At the end of the quick two-minute assessment, students first circle and count the words they thought of independently; then they share their lists with neighboring students to expand their internal word wall and to give them an opportunity to write additional words on their own lists.

This quick preassessment gives teachers an instantaneous look at the students' prior knowledge on that particular topic in a two-minute window. In addition to providing a preassessment, the strategy boosts the immediate oral word knowledge students have, because they have listened to the lists of others.

The interventions at Tiers 2 and 3 are differentiated as well, gradually becoming more and more systematic and explicit. Although they will be used to teach the same content standards or skills that were taught in Tier 1, they must use different strategies or approaches. After all, if the strategy used in Tier 1 had been effective, the student would not need an intervention! As in Tier 1, the teacher documents results from multiple types of assessments and progress monitoring.

Returning to the example of "ABC Brainstorm," students who struggle with vocabulary may need differentiated strategies or Tier 2 targeted interventions. In their book, *Making Words Their Own* (2008), Allen and Nickelsen suggest that it may help English language learners to have the brainstormed words and new vocabulary listed on index cards with illustrations or mnemonics. Dividing each card into quadrants with the vocabulary word in the center helps struggling students who are visual/spatial learners, as they need to see patterns and relationships. Since many students understand new information better when they can compare and contrast "what it is" with "what it is not," adding synonyms and antonyms to the card makes it even clearer. Once they have written the picture or symbol, synonym, and antonym, they are ready to write the definition of the word (see Figure 4.6).

Bodily/kinesthetic learners learn through muscle memory, so having them create a movement for difficult words will help them remember the word's meaning.

Figure 4.6 Sample Index Card for Visual/Spatial Learners

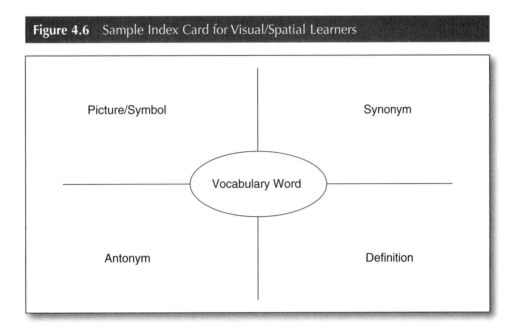

FRAME

In teaching you cannot see the fruit of a day's work. It is invisible and remains so, maybe for twenty years.

—Jacques Barzun

This chapter has explored a variety of ways to be responsive to the needs of teachers and students. By using PLCs as the framework for sharing new strategies and understandings, discussing data collected through assessments, and evaluating data against benchmarks, teachers have a strong support system in which to make their instructional decisions. Within that framework, DI provides the research and strategies to reach and teach today's increasingly diverse student population. And RTI brings colleagues and community members together to help all students be successful.

Nonnegotiables

The nonnegotiables for the integrated model are listed under "What's In" in Table 4.5. If your school still exhibits any behaviors or actions listed under "What's Out," you may have a great place to start weaving your own tapestry!

Table 4.5 What's In—What's Out

What's In	What's Out
• High expectations for all students • Teacher-student conferring and goal setting • Teacher-teacher shared decision making and problem solving • School-family information and consultation • Administrative support for teachers • Unpacking state and national standards with colleagues • Using assessment data to guide instruction and to design interventions • Focusing on high-quality, evidence-based instruction • Differentiating instruction and interventions • Fidelity of implementation • Continuous reflection	• High expectations for only the bright students • Planning and teaching in isolation • Involving family members only when absolutely necessary • Managing through fear and power • Teaching a one-size-fits-all curriculum • Using the textbook as the curriculum • Starting at the standards level rather than working toward the standards level

REFERENCES AND RESOURCES

Allen, L., & Nickelsen, L. (2008). *Making words their own: Building foundations for powerful vocabularies.* Peterborough, NH: Crystal Springs Books.

Allington, R. (2006). Research and the three tier model. *Reading Today, 23*(5), 20.

Batsche, G., Elliott, J., Graden, J. L., Grimes, J., Kovaleski, J. F., Prasse, D., Reschly, D., et al. (2005). *Response to intervention: Policy considerations and implementation.* Alexandria, VA: National Association of State Directors of Special Education.

Bender, W. N., & Shores, C. (2007). *Response to intervention: A practical guide for every teacher.* Thousand Oaks, CA: Corwin.

Blackburn, B. (2008). *Rigor is not a four-letter word.* Larchmont, NY: Eye on Education.

Brown-Chidsey, R. (2007). No more "waiting to fail": How response to intervention works and why it is needed. *Educational Leadership, 65*(2), 40–46.

Brown-Chidsey, R., Bronaugh, L., & McGraw, K. (2009). *RTI in the classroom: Guidelines and recipes for success.* New York: The Guilford Press.

Brown-Chidsey, R., & Steege, M. W. (2005). *Response to intervention: Principles and strategies for effective practice.* New York: The Guilford Press.

Buffum, A., Mattos, M., & Weber, C. (2009). *Pyramid response to intervention: RTI, professional learning communities, and how to respond when kids don't learn.* Bloomington, IN: Solution Tree.

Chafouleas, S., Riley-Tilman, C., & Sugai, G. (2007). *School-based behavior assessment: Informing intervention and instruction.* New York: The Guilford Press.

Costa, A., & Kallick, B. (2000). *Discovering and exploring habits of mind.* Alexandria, VA: ASCD.

Council for Exceptional Children. (2007). *Position on Response to Intervention (RTI): The unique role of special education and special educators* (position statement). Arlington, VA: Author.

DuFour, R., DuFour, R., & Eaker, R. (2008). *Revisiting professional learning communities at work: New insights for improving schools.* Bloomington, IN: Solution Tree.

DuFour, R., & Eaker, R. (1993). *Professional learning communities at work: Best practices for enhancing student achievement.* Bloomington, IN: Solution Tree.

Fisher, D., & Frey, N. (2010). *Enhancing RTI: How to ensure success with effective classroom instruction & intervention.* Alexandria, VA: ASCD.

Fletcher, J. M., Coulter, W. A., Reschly, D. J., & Vaughn, S. (2004). Alternative approaches to the definition and identification of learning disabilities: Some questions and answers. *Annals of Dyslexia, 54*(2), 304–331.

Fogarty, R., & Stoehr, J. (2008). *Integrating curricula with multiple intelligences: Teams, themes & threads.* Thousand Oaks, CA: Corwin.

Freeman, D., & Freeman, Y. (2004). Three types of English language learners. *School Talk: Newsletter of the National Council of Teachers of English, 9*(4), 1–3.

Fuchs, D., & Fuchs, L. S. (2006). Introduction to response to intervention: What, why, and how valid is it? *Reading Research Quarterly, 41*(1), 93–99.

Fuchs, D., Mock, D., Morgan, P. L., & Young, C. L. (2003). Responsiveness-to-intervention: Definitions, evidence, and implications for the learning disabilities construct. *Learning Disabilities: Research & Practice, 18,* 157–171.

Fuchs, L. S., & Fuchs, D. (2007). A model for implementing responsiveness to intervention. *Teaching Exceptional Children, 39*(5), 14–20.

Ginsburg, H. P., & Baroody, A. J. (1990). *Test of early math ability* (3rd ed.) (TEMA-3). Los Angeles: Western Psychological Services.

Haager, D., Dimino, J. A., & Windmueller, M. (2007). *Interventions for reading success.* Baltimore, MD: Paul H Brookes.

Haager, D., Klingner, J., & Vaughn, S. (2007). *Evidence-based reading practices for response to intervention.* Baltimore, MD: Paul H Brookes.

Hawkins, J. D., Catalano, R. F., Kosterman, R., Abbott, R., & Hill, K. (1999). Preventing adolescent health-risk behaviors by strengthening protection during childhood. *Archives of Pediatrics & Adolescent Medicine, 153,* 226–234.

Hayes Jacobs, H. (Ed.) (2010). *Curriculum 21: Essential education for a changing world.* Alexandria, VA: ASCD.

Howard, M. (2009). *RTI from all sides: What every teacher needs to know.* Portsmouth, NH: Heinemann.

Ihnot, C., Mastoff, J., Gavin, J., & Hendrickson, L. (2001). *Read naturally.* St. Paul, MN: Read Naturally.

Individuals with Disabilities Education Act, 20 U.S.C. § 1400.

International Reading Association. (2000). *Making a difference means making it different* (position statement). Newark, DE: Author.

Kame'enui, E. J. (2007). A new paradigm: Responsiveness to intervention. *Teaching Exceptional Children, 39*(5), 6–7.

Kottler, E., Kottler, J. A., & Street, C. (2008). *English language learners in your classroom.* Thousand Oaks, CA: Corwin.

Leslie, L., & Allen, L. (1999). Factors that predict success in an early literacy intervention project. *Reading Research Quarterly, 34*(4), 404–424.

McCook, J. E. (2006). *The RTI guide: Developing and implementing a model in your schools.* Horsham, PA: LRP.

Mellard, D. F., & Johnson, E. (2008). *RTI—A practitioner's guide to implementing response to intervention.* Thousand Oaks, CA: Corwin.

Meyer, M. S. (2000). The ability-achievement discrepancy: Does it contribute to an understanding of learning disabilities? *Educational Psychology Review, 12*(3), 315–337.

National Institute for Child Health and Human Development, Reading, Writing, and Related Learning Disabilities (RWRLD) Program. http://www.nichd.nih .gov/about/org/crmc/cdb/prog_rwrld/index.cfm

National Research Center on Learning Disabilities. (2002). *Common ground report.* Reston, VA: Author.

National Summit on Learning Disabilities: Building a Foundation for the Future. (August, 2001). Washington, DC. http://ldsummit.air.org

O'Connor, R. (2003, December). *Tiers of intervention in kindergarten through third grade.* Paper presented at the Responsiveness-to-Intervention Symposium, Kansas City, MO.

Partnership for 21st Century Skills. (n.d.). *Framework for 21st century learning.* Retrieved from http://www.p21.org/index.php?option=com_content&task= view&id=254&Itemid=119

President's Commission on Excellence in Special Education. (2002). *A new era: Revitalizing special education for children and their families.* Retrieved from www .ed.gov/inits/commissionsboards/index.html

Sousa, D. A. (2009). *How the brain influences behavior: Management strategies for every classroom.* Thousand Oaks, CA: Corwin.

Speece, D. L., Case, L. P., & Molloy, D. E. (2003). Responsiveness to general education instruction as the first gate to learning disabilities identification. *Learning Disabilities: Research and Practice, 18,* 147–156.

The IRIS Center. (2007). *Dialogue guides. Topic: Two approaches to response to intervention (RTI).* Alexandria, VA: National Association of State Directors of Special Education, IDEA Partnership. Retrieved from http://ideapartnership.org/ media/documents/RTI-Collection/beginning/iris_dg_2approach_rti.pdf

Tilly, W. D., III. (2003, December). *How many tiers are needed for successful prevention and early intervention? Heartland Area Education Agency's evolution from four to three tiers.* Paper presented at the Responsiveness-to-Intervention Symposium, Kansas City, MO.

Tomlinson, C.A. (2001). *How to differentiate instruction in mixed-ability classrooms* (2nd ed.). Alexandria, VA: ASCD.

U.S. Department of Education. (2000). *Twenty-second annual report to Congress on the implementation of the Individuals with Disabilities Education Act.* Washington, DC: Author.

U.S. Office of Education. (1977). Assistance to states for education of handicapped children: Procedures for evaluating specific learning disabilities. *Federal Register, 42*, pp. 65082–65085.

Vaughn, S., & Fuchs, L. S. (2003). Redefining learning disabilities as inadequate response to instruction: The promise and potential problems. *Learning Disabilities: Research & Practice, 18*, 137–146.

Wiggins, G., & McTighe, J. (2005). *Understanding by design* (2nd ed.). Alexandria, VA: ASCD.

FURTHER RESOURCES AVAILABLE ONLINE

Aimsweb: Assessment and Data Management for RTI

http://www.aimsweb.com
(curriculum-based measurement tools, data-collection tools, and RTI package; subscription required)

Center for Implementing Technology in Education

http://www.cited.org/index.aspx?page_id=8
(tools for integrating instructional technology for all students to achieve high educational standards)

Florida State University (Behavioral Interventions page)

http://www.fsu.edu/~truancy/interventions.html
(behavior interventions)

Intervention Central

http://www.interventioncentral.org
(curriculum-based assessments and tools)

MoraModules

http://moramodules.com/
(modules for teaching English language learners)

National Center for Culturally Responsive Educational Systems

http://www.nccrest.org
(strategies and information for English language learners, African Americans)

National Center on Response to Intervention

http://www.rti4success.org
(questions and answers for selecting progress monitoring tools)

RTI Tools: A Response to Intervention Directory

http://www.rtitools.com/Progress_Monitoring/Tools/
(overview of components of progress monitoring tools)

U.S. Department of Education. Building the Legacy: IDEA 2004

http://idea.ed.gov/explore/view/p/,root,dynamic,QaCorner,8
(overview of RTI, statutes)

5 Weaving a Tapestry for School Change

I've come to the frightening conclusion that I am the decisive element in the classroom. It is my daily mood that makes the weather. As a teacher I possess a tremendous power to make a child's life miserable or joyous. I can be a tool of torture or an instrument of inspiration. I can humiliate or humor, hurt or heal. In all situations it is my response that decides whether a crisis will be escalated or deescalated and a child humanized or dehumanized.

—Haim Ginott

Not all of us are at the same place during the same season. There will always be issues that cause us as teachers, parents, and administrators to be at different places emotionally, socially, and professionally.

That said . . . it is reasonable to be concerned that not all stakeholders are willing to participate in improving the climate of your school. Their reasons—no matter how many—almost always boil down to three major issues: time, money, and commitment.

TIME

Time is free, but it is priceless. You can't own it but you can use it. You can't keep it, but you can spend it. Once you've lost it you can never get it back.

—Harvey Mackay

There will always be individuals with the following concerns relating to time:

- We don't have time to do all of this.
- We don't have collaborative planning time.
- We can't stay after school, because everyone has something else to do.

To get started, actively look for other individuals within your professional community with whom you can have conversations about teaching and learning. Not everyone needs to be involved in the initial implementation. Start small, with those who are interested in improving their practice. People have to catch the fever.

Simple Ways to Get Started

Professional Learning Communities

Find a colleague or two with whom you can

- have dialogues about student work and artifacts.
- share a favorite piece of literature.
- share a quote that is meaningful to your profession and your life.
- relate something that has worked in your classroom.

Differentiated Instruction

A few things that might help you get started with differentiated instruction include the following:

- Observe your students' behavior, and plot their learner profiles in the "file cabinet" on Laura Candler's Teaching Resources website, www.lauracandler.com/filecabinet.
- Have older students complete a multiple intelligences inventory on Walter McKenzie's One and Only Surfaquarium, http://surfaquarium .com/MI/index.htm.
- Investigate the aspects of cooperative learning by viewing a free Spencer Kagan podcast at tvo.org (search the site for "Spencer Kagan"), or look for him at www.kaganonline.com.
- Go to TeacherTube.com and find a differentiated lesson. As you watch, complete double entry notes (what I noticed—what I want to try).

- Make a list of what you have taught and what your students need to learn. Discuss with a colleague the instructional strategies that seemed to work best for your students and what patterns you noticed.

Response to Intervention

Instruction and intervention in the RTI framework are designed to help struggling students gain positive momentum within the classroom. Use the following ideas to support that momentum:

- Bring unidentified student work to a meeting, and exchange your students' work samples with those of a colleague. Use a T-chart to list or map out what each of you notices about the other's samples as they compare to an appropriate rubric or checklist and what strategies you would recommend for further instruction.
- With your colleague(s), discuss the support systems that are already in place for your students. Identify types of groupings you use in class (flexible, guided, independent conference, etc.), and analyze how you use peer partnerships to meet student learning goals.
- Develop a list with your colleague(s) of people who can support you in meeting specific student needs.
- With a colleague, create intervention planning sheets for academics and behavior that include the following:
  o Student strengths
  o Any individualized information that is not in each student's cumulative folder
  o Previous interventions and the corresponding results
  o Ongoing interventions that are currently in place
  o Any problematic behaviors that occur outside the classroom for the student
  o Replacement behaviors (What behaviors would you like to see the student be able to use to replace misbehaviors? Think SMART: specific, measurable, attainable, realistic, and timely.)
  o Other pertinent information

MONEY

They deem me mad because I will not sell my days for gold; and I deem them mad because they think my days have a price.

—Kahlil Gibran

Just as there are those who are concerned about time, money is also an issue for many educators. When considering change, the first questions they ask are the following:

- How much will this cost?
- What if our school has no money?
- Where will we find the money?

Table 5.1 lists a variety of lower- and higher-cost suggestions for initiating, implementing, and sustaining change around professional learning communities, differentiated instruction, and response to intervention.

Table 5.1 Lower- and Higher-Cost Suggestions for Implementing PLCs, DI, and RTI

Lower Cost	Higher Cost

• Check your state or local educational agencies for free programs and services that will help improve teaching and learning. Online examples include the following:
 	
  o www.cciu.org
  o www.PaTTAN.net
 	
• Join professional organizations such as IRA, ASCD, NAPSE, and NSDC.
• Use professional journals and magazines such as *Educational Leadership* for discussions on relevant, current issues of school reform.
• Buy a book, and share it with colleagues.
• Facilitate collegial conversations.
• Conduct a book study.
• Apply for a small grant from your local education foundation, or try www.donorschoice.com.
• Showcase best practices by educators in your school throughout the year.
• Have teachers visit each other's classrooms.
• Use reflection journals.
	• Procure an outside consultant for professional development.
	• Send a team to America's Choice (www.americaschoice.org).
	• Send teachers or administrators to a state or national conference.
	• Enroll in online courses at various colleges and universities.
	• Establish a video library of best practices.
	• Become a member of a larger project, such as the National Writing Project (www.nwp.org).
	• Become a member of a consortium on
	
	  o Minority student achievement
	  o Technology
	  o Professional learning communities
	  o Other

COMMITMENT

The man who removes a mountain begins by carrying away small stones.

—Chinese proverb

In a revision of a 1997 report, the National Institute of Standards and Technology explains that although Congress passed the Metric Conversion Act of 1975 to increase the use of the metric system in the United States, it created little change. The U.S. Metric Board was charged with carrying out a broad program of planning, coordination, and public education to assist in making the changes across the country; however, by 1981, the board reported that its efforts were largely ignored by the American public. This public included many school teachers who refused to teach it. They simply were not willing or ready to commit to such a major change.

When discussing degrees of commitment, oft-heard statements include the following:

- I don't know what to do first.
- Change is overwhelming.
- I have too much on my plate to start something new.
- My administrator is [or my colleagues are] undermining my efforts.
- I don't really understand this well enough to implement it.

In response to these concerns regarding commitment to change (and with respect to Costa and Kallick (2000) in adapting some of their Habits of Mind), here are some things educators can do:

- Create a big picture organizer in order to see where you are going. Start small, focusing on one component at a time. Be accurate. Just as we work with students to reach mastery, so should we practice instructional strategies for mastery for the good of the students.
- Think flexibly, and know that decisions you make within your PLC and within your individual classrooms do change, even when those first decisions are made with intent.
- Find like-minded individuals with whom to collaborate. Use each other as sounding boards to question your choice of strategies, analysis of data, goals, learning profiles, and so forth.
- Look for a neutral place of mutual support, either in or out of the school building, that exudes safety and respect with regard to all in attendance, for example, a local cafe, bookstore, town library, school library, or board room.

- Listen with understanding and empathy as others share their views, prior knowledge, strategies, issues, and struggles as you begin to support one another in the work of a professional learning community.
- Continue professional and independent learning through reading, research, conversation, colleague observations, and attending professional development opportunities when possible.
- Laugh with one another. Find the humor in your profession, in your students, and in yourself. Make your classroom a place where you want to be and your students feel compelled to be.

When colleagues have the attitude that "this too shall pass" or "something else will come along to replace this," what they're really feeling is (1) a lack of self-respect, (2) a lack of buy-in, and (3) a concern that their voices are not being heard. Because new initiatives have occurred so often, teachers' memories of new ideas that have come and gone sometimes block any interest they may have in seriously committing to any new initiative. This lack of interest is often a façade that is used as an excuse not to participate by individuals who are fearful, who suffer from feelings of inadequacy, or who may simply lack pedagogy and content knowledge.

In order to support these colleagues, we must try to understand and empathize with them. We must help them understand that many aspects of education are somewhat cyclical, in that we build on what has been done in the past with new brain research and evidence-based strategies. Instead of asking them to throw the baby out with the bath water, how can we use what they are already doing as examples to convince them to change one concept, strategy, or component of instruction or assessment at a time to find their hidden potential?

Throughout this text we have provided practical strategies to be examined, implemented, and integrated into PLCs, DI, and RTI. We are firm believers that empowerment begins with knowledge, conviction, practice, and passion for what you do each and every day. Change *can and does* occur. Children *can and do* learn. Teachers *can and do* embrace change when they are given time, voice, and choice as well as opportunities to develop and demonstrate leadership skills. Please use this text to begin your journey for initiating and managing change within yourself, your classroom, and your school community. Feel free to contact us with your stories about change or with questions you have about implementing reform in your school or weaving your own tapestry through professional development.

REFERENCES AND RESOURCES

Costa, A., & Kallick, B. (2000). *Discovering and exploring habits of mind.* Alexandria, VA: Association for Supervision and Curriculum Development.

National Institute of Standards and Technology. (1997/2002). *The United States and the metric system: a capsule history.* Retrieved from www.nist.gov/pml/wmd/metric/upload/1136a.pdf

Appendix A

Forms and Templates

Professional Learning Communities Survey

This survey will help you begin to think about and assess the extent to which each of the major factors associated with professional learning communities is currently present at your school.

Rate your district/building readiness for PLCs according to the following scale:

- Not developed = 0
- Partially developed = 1
- Fully developed = 2

	Rating	Comments
1. Faculty and staff members talk with each other about their teaching situations and the specific, daily challenges they face.		
2. Teachers in our school share, observe, and discuss pedagogy and each others' teaching methods or philosophies.		
3. Teachers assume that all students can learn at reasonably high levels and that teachers can help them.		
4. Teachers not only work together to develop shared understandings of students, curriculum, and instructional policy, but also produce evidence-based materials or activities that improve instruction, curriculum, and assessment.		
5. The building administrator participates democratically with staff in meetings and decisions, sharing power and authority.		
6. The building administrator is familiar with the critical elements of learning communities.		
7. Teachers take risks in trying evidence-based techniques and ideas and in making efforts to learn more about their profession.		
8. Teachers feel honored for their capabilities within the school as well as within the district, the parent community, and other significant groups.		

(Continued)

(Continued)

	Rating	Comments
9. Within the school, there are formal methods for sharing expertise among faculty members so that teachers can improve.		
10. The school leadership keeps the school focused on shared purpose, continuous improvement, and collaboration.		
11. There is a formal process that provides substantial and regularly scheduled blocks of time for educators to conduct ongoing self-examination and self-renewal.		
12. Teachers have common spaces, rooms, or areas for discussion of educational practices.		
13. There are recurring formal situations in which teachers work together to plan and integrate lessons for team teaching.		
14. There are structures and opportunities for an exchange of ideas, both within and across such organizational units as teams, grade levels, and subject departments.		
15. Teachers have autonomy to make decisions regarding their work guided by the norms and beliefs of the professional community.		
16. Professional development addresses critical elements of effective implementation of professional learning communities, such as A. using data to inform instruction. B. evidence-based instructional practices. C. protocols and procedures involving screening and progress monitoring. D. 21st century literacy skills. E. comprehensive literacy. F. differentiated instruction. G. curriculum-based measurement instruments. H. math snapshots. I. collaborative teaming. J. lesson studies.		

Source: Adapted from Kruse, Louis, & Bryk (1994).

Needs Assessment for Differentiated Professional Development

This needs assessment survey is designed to obtain input on your professional development needs. (1 is strongly disagree and 4 is strongly agree.)

PLEASE RETURN COMPLETED SURVEY TO: _____

1. Professional development in which I have participated in the last year has been

linked to other improvement programs at my school.	1	2	3	4
provided via coaching.	1	2	3	4
followed up by administrative or collegial support.	1	2	3	4

2. Currently, I feel well prepared to implement the following:

reading/writing workshop	1	2	3	4
core curriculum standards	1	2	3	4
evidence-based practices, such as differentiation of instruction	1	2	3	4
intervention strategies	1	2	3	4
strategies that support the needs of students with limited English proficiency	1	2	3	4

3. As a result of my recent professional development experiences, my students

are more interested and motivated to learn.	1	2	3	4
demonstrate greater contextual understanding.	1	2	3	4
are better able to apply critical thinking.	1	2	3	4
are better able to work collaboratively.	1	2	3	4

4. Professional development in the following areas would benefit me:

content—subject-specific	1	2	3	4
evidence-based teaching practices	1	2	3	4
discipline or management	1	2	3	4
assessment	1	2	3	4
technology	1	2	3	4
personalized professional development of my choice	1	2	3	4

5. I believe the ideal time for professional development would be

early morning before school.	1	2	3	4
during the school day.	1	2	3	4
after school.	1	2	3	4

Evaluation for Teacher Effectiveness
Self-Efficacy for Teaching

Grade _____ Date _____

Directions to teachers: In the section below, please indicate HOW MUCH YOU AGREE OR DISAGREE with each of the statements. (1 is strongly disagree and 5 is strongly agree.)

1. I feel that I make an educational difference in the lives of my students. 1 2 3 4 5
2. If I try really hard, I can get through to even the most difficult students. 1 2 3 4 5
3. A student's school *motivation* depends on the home environment. 1 2 3 4 5
4. I am able to work with students of different ages and abilities. 1 2 3 4 5
5. I am successful with all the students in my class. 1 2 3 4 5
6. I am uncertain how to teach and reach some of my students. 1 2 3 4 5
7. I feel as though some of my students are not making academic progress. 1 2 3 4 5
8. My students' peers influence their *motivation* more than I do. 1 2 3 4 5
9. Most of a student's *performance* depends on the home environment. 1 2 3 4 5
10. My students' *performance* is influenced by their peers. 1 2 3 4 5
11. I feel as though I have enough knowledge of pedagogy to support my students. 1 2 3 4 5
12. My interpersonal relationships with administrators are positive. 1 2 3 4 5
13. My interpersonal relationships with colleagues are strong. 1 2 3 4 5
14. I am a part of a healthy school environment. 1 2 3 4 5
15. At my school, the teachers, principals, and school professionals trust each other. 1 2 3 4 5
16. In planning my professional development, I choose items that . . . (circle all that apply)

engage me in conversation.   allow me to work by myself.   permit me to see or view the demonstration.

involve me in an active, hands-on fashion.   afford me opportunities to listen to lectures.   other

Teacher Survey About Writing

This survey will provide benchmarks for thinking through what is needed for teachers and students to thrive in the writing environment. Please read and answer the questions. (1 is strongly disagree and 5 is strongly agree.)

Name _____ Position _____

1. I know what is expected of me regarding the teaching of writing.   1   2   3   4   5

2. I have the materials and equipment I need to do my work.   1   2   3   4   5

3. I am aware of the elements of the writing continuum.   1   2   3   4   5

4. In the last year, I have used student writing to inform my instruction.   1   2   3   4   5

5. My students believe that they are writers.   1   2   3   4   5

6. My students see and understand the importance of writing in daily life.   1   2   3   4   5

7. I share my writing with my students.   1   2   3   4   5

8. I have a writing mentor.   1   2   3   4   5

9. My students have writing mentors.   1   2   3   4   5

10. I use mentor/touchstone text to teach and promote writing.   1   2   3   4   5

11. The most difficult aspect of teaching writing is . . .

12. Teaching writing is like . . .

13. During PLC conversations, I would like to learn . . . (check all that apply)

 ☐ how to manage my writing block.

 ☐ how to develop minilessons for writing workshop.

 ☐ how to effectively use mentor text for writing.

 ☐ about writing to learn (content area strategies).

 ☐ other techniques to support writers.

 ☐ (other) _____

Measuring Rigor

Take time to reflect about the lesson you planned. Use the following scale when answering the questions:

    1 = Strongly agree ("For the most part, yes.")
    2 = Agree ("Yes, but . . .")
    3 = Disagree ("No, but . . .")
    4 = Strongly disagree ("For the most part, no.")
    5 = Not applicable to this lesson

Complexity	Emotion
To what extent is the lesson organized around complex, interrelated concepts? 1 2 3 4 5	To what extent does the lesson arouse strong feelings and discussion among students? 1 2 3 4 5
Provocation	**Ambiguity**
To what extent is the lesson concerned with central problems in the discipline that challenge students' previous concepts? 1 2 3 4 5	To what extent does the lesson focus on symbols and images packed with multiple meanings? 1 2 3 4 5

Comments

_____

_____

_____

_____

Source: Adapted from Strong, Silver, & Perini (2001).

Interest and Learning Profile Inventory
What I Would Like to Learn More About
(for Middle School and High School)

Name: _____

If you could choose what you would get to learn about this year, what three things would you choose?

I would like to have a chance to learn about

    1.

    2.

    3.

What three ways do you learn best?

    1.

    2.

    3.

Have you ever visited an art gallery or art museum? YES _____ NO _____

If you have visited an art museum, was there a particular kind of art or an artist that you especially liked? _____

Have you ever attended a musical concert? YES _____ NO _____

Do you play a musical instrument? YES _____ NO _____

If you play a musical instrument, what one do you play? _____

If you do not play an instrument, what one would you enjoy learning to play?

_____

What are your favorite sports? _____

Do you have any sports heroes? _____

What kind of animals do you enjoy or find to be interesting? _____

What are your two favorite hobbies? _____

Differentiation of Instruction Walk-Through Checklist

This checklist is designed to assist schools in the assessment of current implementation of evidence-based differentiation of instruction. Data generated using this checklist may be used in the design of professional learning. The dialogue generated from sharing the data will inform teacher practice and build consensus for deep, schoolwide understanding and change.

Teacher:	Walk Through:	Observer:		
Content Area:	Grade Level:	Time in: _____ Time Out: _____		
Content	**Possible Observations/Artifacts**	**Evident?**		**Comments**
*Addressing student needs by strategically **adapting the depth, pace, and delivery mode** of what is taught and providing **various avenues for students to access** the content while still aligning to the curriculum standard(s)*	• assignments of differing depth, complexity, or resources • curriculum compacting, eliminating work on content that has been mastered and streamlining instruction to a pace commensurate with students' readiness • reteaching to small groups based on data gathered from formative assessment • evidence of making content accessible through various means—audio/video of written content, graphic organizers, use of manipulatives, peer partnerships • student oral and written responses that reveal that content is accessible • anchor charts (which leave evidence of learning), documents, or learning station materials that indicate modification of content to ensure equitable access to learning • other: _____	Yes No Some evidence NA		
Process	**Possible Observations/Artifacts**	**Evident?**		**Comments**
*Addressing student needs by **strategically creating student learning***	• assignments or parallel tasks at varied difficulty levels: materials eliminated or accelerated; activities designed to teach, for practice, or to reteach	Yes No Some evidence NA		

(Continued)

(Continued)

experiences that allow for **differing student processes,** while still aligning to all elements of the curriculum standard(s)	• tasks that are matched in complexity to student understanding and skill: respectful, busy, and engaging • evidence of matching activity to student learning style or modality: "Symphony," "Partner Talk" • activities that require using essential skills or information to answer an essential question that include varying levels of scaffolding (support) and a method for proving individual mastery: "Ticket Into Class," read-write-pair-share, "Exit Ticket," "Yesterday's News," evidence of learning logs, graphic organizers, role playing, learning stations, model making, and/or labs, task cards, independent tasks. • other: _____		
Product	**Possible Observations/Artifacts**	**Evident?**	**Comments**
Addressing student needs by **strategically designing student performance tasks** that will result in differing **student work products,** while still aligning to all elements of the curriculum standard(s)	• performance tasks designed with clear, incremental requirements, accessible to all learners • evidence of materials in students' primary languages and/or strong system in place for language acquisition—pictures, graphics, and peer support • tasks that require students to rethink, use, and extend what they have learned over a long period of time, student-created products that show evidence of learning • opportunity for students to go public, presenting information to diverse and appropriate audiences • initial and ongoing assessments of student readiness and growth (formative and summative), evidence of an assessment plan for differentiated assessment	Yes No Some evidence NA	

		Evident?	Comments
	• student goal setting using SMART goals methods • evidence of use of technology and multimedia resources • other: _____		

Learning Environment	Possible Observations/Artifacts	Evident?	Comments
*Addressing student needs by strategically **adjusting the learning environment** (physical space, protocols/ structures, furniture, materials, time allotted for activities), while still instructing all students for mastery of standard(s)*	• established protocols for students to efficiently transition to and operate within different work configurations: menus, contracts, cues, discussion, management boards • classroom areas for quiet study or listening, vocabulary development (with charts and skills-related games), writing and responding, investigation, peer discussion, and teacher demonstration • adjusted time for some students and/ or student groups to complete a given work task • student negotiation and discussion of the need for adjusting assignments or tasks • flexibility that allows for changes to grouping, seating, materials, time, or structures as student needs change • differing teacher feedback that addresses the needs of specific students or student groups • nonvisible learning environment made palpable (by communicated high expectations, positive interactions, risk-free learning climate) • other: _____	Yes No Some evidence NA	

Data Source for DI	Possible Observations/Artifacts	Evident in this visit?	
Readiness Level: *use of academic diagnostic data to inform differentiation*	• small group instruction (groups determined by readiness): demonstrations; modeling; practice provided in peer partnerships, with the classroom teacher, and/or an aide or volunteer	Yes No Some evidence NA	

(Continued)

(Continued)

	• homework options and scaffolded assignments: menus, task boards, tic-tac-toe charts, or learning modalities related to assignments • formative assessments to determine readiness: "Exit Ticket," "Take a Stand," "Reflect and Retell"; graphic organizers: Venn diagram, matrix, continuums, sequential organizers • negotiated criteria: peer partnerships, think-pair-preview-postview mentorships • activities observed from list above used to differentiate for ____ content ____ process ____ product ____ learning environment	
Learning Styles: *use of data regarding each student's most effective learning style to inform differentiation*	• learning style inventory responses administered, and subsequent lessons • incorporate student learning interests • encourage students to help create tasks and define products based on learning style • are adjusted for student learning style • establish clear criteria for success • adjust work time based on student readiness, interest, and learning style • teacher aware of student cues so she or he can adjust instruction accordingly; documents and describes student learning relative to concept development, reading, social interaction, and communication skills • student choices include enrichment or accelerated study, encourage students to help create tasks and define products • activities observed from list above used to differentiate for ____ content ____ process ____ product ____ learning environment	Yes No Some evidence NA

Interests: use of data regarding collective and individual interests to inform differentiation	<ul><li>interest inventory responses</li><li>student choice based on interest; all students have the opportunity to work with other students who are similar to and dissimilar from themselves in terms of interest, readiness, and learning profile</li><li>student and teacher discussions include accountable talk, put forth and demand knowledge that is accurate and relevant to the issue under discussion</li><li>"bridging" of familiar ideas and experiences to academic content</li><li>activities observed from list above used to differentiate for ____ content ____ process ____ product ____ learning environment</li></ul>	Yes No Some evidence NA
Student Personal Goals: use of student-established and articulated goals to inform differentiation of instruction	<ul><li>written student goals; SMART goals used and students are an integral part of goal setting</li><li>spoken student goals with individual goal setting and conferencing before, during, and after teaching; teacher feels that students will "self-differentiate" when given choices</li><li>student responsibility contracts designed so that students function at the academic levels most suitable to them and work with resource materials containing concepts and knowledge that are appropriate to their abilities and experiences</li><li>data walls, portfolios, goal sheets, progress charts with student goals "starred" or otherwise marked</li><li>activities observed from list above used to differentiate for ____ content ____ process ____ product ____ learning environment</li></ul>	Yes No Some evidence NA

Differentiation of Instruction
Teacher Readiness Survey

The purpose of the following survey is to determine the degree to which you are familiar with, ready for, and differentiating instruction in your classroom. The results of this anonymous survey will be used to guide professional development.

Grade level (position) _____

Content area(s) you teach (if applicable) _____

Number of years teaching _____

Rate your district/building readiness for DI according to the following scale:

- Not ready = 0
- Partially developed = 1
- Fully developed = 2

	Rating	Comments
1. I have attended at least three trainings on differentiation of instruction.		
2. I have received an overview of the DI concept, understand its general features, and know how DI differs from traditional approaches.		
3. I have had organized discussions regarding the need for and integration of DI into current school practices, and we have begun to develop a written plan.		
4. I understand that DI is not something additional that we do. DI is a pedagogical shift and a change in the way we do things.		
5. I understand that DI is embedded in general education, not special education.		
6. I understand that DI helps all children—struggling learners, average learners, and advanced learners.		
7. I use personal observations and classroom assessments to help guide my decisions about differentiating instruction for students.		
8. I make adjustments in time and pacing to accommodate learners with special needs.		

9. I develop assignments that challenge and expand students' interests.		
10. I plan assignments that reflect individual student learning styles.		
11. I communicate with other school staff with regard to instruction, intervention, and data collection.		
12. I apply real-life situations to lesson plans.		
13. I use curriculum compacting (pretesting students before a unit and then eliminating instruction in areas of competence).		
14. My school has put together a library of effective evidence-based ideas for differentiation of instruction.		
15. I believe that my school has developed a series of methods of formative and summative assessment to track student progress and drive instruction.		
16. My school will follow up with me soon after differentiation has been put into place to ensure that I am able to get started and to provide support.		
17. I use learning stations, student choice, and flexible grouping as part of my daily instruction.		
18. In daily instruction, I use instructional materials for the same lesson that vary according to student readiness, interest, cultural differences, or other area of student difference.		
19. I vary grouping structures (ability, cross-ability, interest, learning profile, random) to facilitate both learning and positive social interaction.		
20. I need professional development that addresses critical elements of DI implementation such as A. using data to inform instruction. B. evidence-based instructional practices. C. formative assessments. D. differentiated instruction. E. math snapshots. F. collaborative scoring. G. tiering and compacting. H. grouping and management.		

Response to Intervention Teacher Readiness Survey

The purpose of the following survey is to determine the degree to which you are familiar with, ready for, and incorporating response to intervention. The results of this anonymous survey will be used to guide professional development.

Grade level (position) _____

Content area(s) you teach (if applicable) _____

Number of years teaching _____

Rate your district/building readiness for RTI according to the following scale:

- Not ready = 0
- Partially developed = 1
- Fully developed = 2

	Rating	Comments
1. I have attended at least three trainings on RTI.		
2. I have received an overview of the RTI model, understand its general features, and know how RTI differs from the traditional "test discrepancy" approach.		
3. I have had organized discussions with colleagues regarding the need for and integration of RTI into current school practices, and we have begun to develop a written plan.		
4. I understand that RTI is not something additional that we do. RTI is a process and a change in the way we do things.		
5. I understand that RTI is embedded in general education, not special education.		
6. I understand that RTI helps all children—struggling learners, average learners, and advanced learners.		
7. I am provided time and resources for data collection and management, including universal screening and progress monitoring.		
8. My school has a core team of individuals representing a variety of roles and related services that meets on a regular basis to discuss student learning. Discussions are not limited to the issues of specific students or a desire for evaluation for special education placement.		
9. My school uses student learning outcomes to collect data and drive decision making.		
10. Goal setting and graphing of student progress is an expected practice in my school.		

11. In my school there is ongoing communication among all personnel with regard to instruction, intervention, and data collection.		
12. My school has inventoried schoolwide resources that it can use in interventions.		
13. My school has developed a series of methods of assessment (e.g., curriculum-based measurement, AIMS Web [Assessment and Data Management], DRA [Developmental Reading Assessment], standardized tests, and DIBELS [Dynamic Indicators of Basic Early Literacy Skills]) to track student progress during the interventions.		
14. My school has put together a library of effective, research-based intervention ideas for common student referral concerns.		
15. My school has put together a series of intervention strategies in step-by-step teacher-friendly verbiage containing enough detail so that educators can easily understand how to put them into practice.		
16. My school follows up with teachers soon after an intervention has been put into place to ensure that the instructor has been able to start the intervention and is being supported.		
17. My school has developed, implemented, and scored curriculum-based measurement instruments in basic skill areas: reading, fluency, math computation, science, social studies, and writing.		
18. My school has developed forms to allow instructors to evaluate student behaviors.		
19. My school has the capabilities to mine data and convert progress-monitoring data into visual displays such as time graphs to aid in instructional and behavioral decision making.		
20. Professional development at my school addresses critical elements of effective RTI implementation, such as A. using data to inform instruction. B. evidence-based instructional practices. C. protocols and procedures involving screening and progress monitoring. D. constructed responses. E. informal reading assessments. F. differentiated instruction. G. curriculum-based measurement instruments. H. math snapshots. I. collaborative teaming. J. lesson studies.		

SMART Goals Action Plan

1. State the goal in SMART format.

Specific: _____

Measurable: _____

Achievable: _____

Results oriented: _____

Target date: _____

2. Describe the data that indicate the need for the goal.

3. Identify the correlation of the stated school improvement goal to the strategic plan.

Check all that apply:

☐ Improve all student performance.

☐ Enhance student social, emotional, and behavioral development.

☐ Develop a diverse workplace that utilizes evidence-based practices.

☐ Promote reliability, competence, responsiveness, and collaboration.

☐ Other: _____

4. Summarize how this goal will be measured. What will be the evidence of goal attainment?

Work Plan

Purpose: To create a "script" for your improvement effort and support implementation.

Directions:

1. Using this form as a template, develop a work plan for each goal identified through the needs assessment process. Modify the form as needed to fit your unique context.

2. Distribute copies of each work plan to the members of the collaboration.

3. Keep copies handy to bring to meetings to review and update regularly. You may decide to develop new work plans for new phases of your reform effort.

Goal:

Results/Accomplishments:

Action Steps *What will be done?*	**Responsibilities** *Who will do it?*	**Time Line** *By when? (day/ month)*	**Resources** *A. Resources available* *B. Resources needed (financial, human, political, and other)*	**Potential Barriers** *A. What individuals or organizations might resist?* *B. How?*	**Communications Plan** *Who is involved? What methods? How often?*
Step 1:			A. B.	A. B.	
Step 2:			A. B.	A. B.	
Step 3:			A. B.	A. B.	
Step 4:			A. B.	A. B.	
Step 5:			A. B.	A. B.	

Evidence of Success: (How will you know that you are making progress? What are your benchmarks?)

Evaluation Process: (How will you determine that your goal has been reached? What are your measures?)

ABC Brainstorm

I know that I know something about . . .

A	N
B	O
C	P
D	Q
E	R
F	S
G	T
H	U
I	V
J	W
K	X
L	Y
M	Z

Teacher to Teacher Walk-Through Protocol

T-Chart	
Noticings	**Teaching Implications**

Tools of the Trade

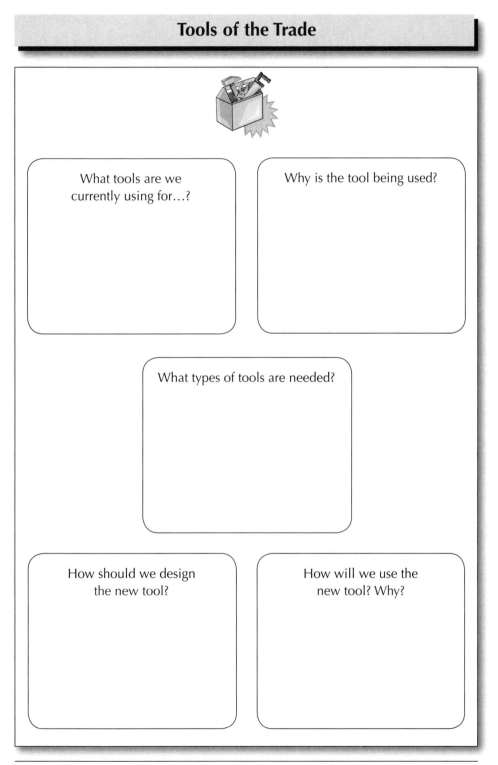

What tools are we currently using for…?

Why is the tool being used?

What types of tools are needed?

How should we design the new tool?

How will we use the new tool? Why?

Kid Watching

Student: _____ Date: _____ Time: _____

Class: _____

Behaviors on which to comment—make a tick mark on the continuum to represent the behavior displayed:

◄───►

off task   on task

◄───►

uncooperative with group members   cooperative with group members

◄───►

overactive with kinesthetic activities   appropriately active

◄───►

blurts answers or interrupts   waits for turn or raises hand

◄───►

hesitant to enter discussion/activity   enthusiastically discusses and
                                                            participates

◄───►

seems unable to hear instructions   follows instructions

◄───►

does not reflect on the ideas of others   reflects on the ideas of others

◄───►

overtly anxious, worried   calm, self-assured learner

Use state and district standards for academic guidelines for your anecdotal notes.

Appendix B

Activities and Protocols

Protocols are a set of structures that individuals use to communicate with one another. Each outlines a code of conduct and is organized to reflect its individual purpose. Information exchanged during a protocol can assist in solving problems related to group functions and communication, as well as teaching and learning issues.

Bull's-Eye Protocol

This is a structured process for helping an individual or teams think more expansively. During this protocol, PLC members reflect on a specific accomplishment to determine whether they have spent enough time turning their goals into reality. They review and modify each goal as needed, using three words to provide a focus for discussion: First, is it *attainable?* Second, is it *precise?* And third, is it *timely* (A.P.T.)?

Number of Participants: small group of no more than 20

Required Time: 30 minutes to several meetings

Step 1

- A PLC is formed within a school.
- Educators with the same collegial focus come together.
- The group decides on meeting dates and times.
- The PLC convenes.

Step 2

- Introductions: Participants introduce themselves if they are not on the same teaching team or do not teach the same grade or content or work within the same school.
- Small group formation: Participants form into groups of two to four.
- Brainstorm: Groups brainstorm ideas for their focus or their time together (e.g., student work, sharing teaching ideas, reflection, etc.). The brainstorming should last 15 to 20 minutes.

Step 3

- At the end of the brainstorming, the entire group reconvenes.
- Participants share some of their small group conversations.
- This discussion should last 5 minutes.

The next two steps aid the group in weeding similar items out of the brainstormed lists, targeting the attainable, and developing a clear-cut plan.

Step 4

- Participants each receive a bull's-eye target (see Figure B.1). They write three specific areas on which they would like to focus their efforts.
- This portion of the protocol should last 10 minutes.

Figure B.1 Bull's-Eye Target

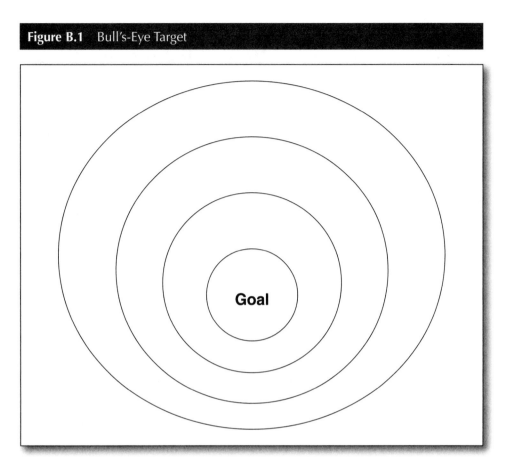

Step 5

- When participants have completed their bull's-eyes, the group reconvenes, and the facilitator collects the targets and aids in prioritizing chosen topics by asking participants to delete items that appear more than once. After the redundant items are cast out, participants rank topics that are most important.
- This should take 15 to 30 minutes.

Step 6

- The facilitator constructs a list of the focus items.
- Participants rank the items by indicating subjects that are most important to address.
- Participants then discuss the process and content of the Bull's-Eye Protocol.

Looking Back Protocol

The purpose of this protocol is for teachers to reflect on individual, student, or schoolwide accomplishments in order to have a clearer understanding of what is needed to continue development. Prior to the meeting, participants write about the work they have done to move forward. During the meeting, they share their written reflections with partners, taking turns to respond. They then share commonalities with the whole group.

The protocol can be used to deepen understanding of student development as well. PLC groups might wish to use this protocol to study student writing or behaviors.

Number of Participants: small groups of 4, 6, or 8.

Required Time: 30 minutes to 1 hour

A facilitator is chosen by the group prior to the session. This individual can be the team leader, classroom teacher, or any member of an existing PLC. He or she assists the group in remaining focused on the time and the issue being discussed.

Step 1—Introduction

- The facilitator introduces the protocol and reminds participants that the purpose of the session is reflection and analysis.

Step 2—Partners

- Participants pair up and share their written reflections.
- During their discussions, partners look for common threads and focus on the ease or difficulty of the reflection itself.
- The discussion should last 10 to 15 minutes.

Step 3—Whole Group

- At the end of the allotted time, the whole group reconvenes.
- Pairs take turns sharing statements about their reflective conversations.
- The sharing should last 5 minutes.

Step 4—Open Discussion

- The facilitator begins this portion by asking participants to participate in an open discussion. They may use the following prompt to begin the focus: "As you look back at the work you have been doing. . . ."
  - What have you learned about yourself through this process?
  - What bumps in the road have you encountered on your journey?
  - What are the differences between the way you approach teaching now and your teaching in the past?
  - What have you learned about your students?
  - What evidence do you have of your new learning?
- This portion of the discussion should last 10 minutes.

Step 5—Debriefing

- In this final part of the process, participants reflect in writing about the following:
  - What they have discovered about themselves, the issue, or the student
  - What they still need to learn
  - What questions the discussion raised

R.I.C.E. (Restate, Illustrate, Compare, and Explain) Protocol

This protocol provides teachers a structure through which they can solve problems related to either the content they teach or the real world. The graphic organizer can be used to arrange content or information in a specific manner in order to uncover the basis of a particular issue related to teaching and/or collaborating. This creative approach to problem solving heightens teacher responsiveness to examining, unraveling, and explaining dilemmas and providing feedback. This protocol is effective both in PLCs and as a classroom strategy.

Number of Participants: works well with any size group

Required Time: 1 hour

A facilitator is chosen by the group prior to the session. This individual can be the team leader, classroom teacher, or any member of an existing PLC. He or she assists the group in remaining focused on the time and the issue being discussed.

Step 1

- The facilitator explains the acronym R.I.C.E to the group.
- The facilitator models the protocol. The following math problem works well for this purpose.

$2 \times 6 = 12$

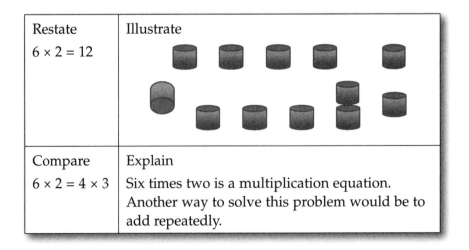

Restate	Illustrate
$6 \times 2 = 12$	
Compare	Explain
$6 \times 2 = 4 \times 3$	Six times two is a multiplication equation. Another way to solve this problem would be to add repeatedly.

Step 2

- The facilitator asks participants to brainstorm other ways that the graphic can be used. If the group cannot come up with the idea to use the organizer for solving personal problems, the facilitator may supply this response.
- The facilitator instructs participants to look back in their journals for a problem that they have attempted to solve related to the content they teach.
- Participants take 5 minutes to share their identified problems with other group members around them, or with a partner.
- The partners/participants then select someone from the small group to share his or her problem with the whole group.
- The facilitator asks the group to restate the information shared.
- This discussion should last 10 to 15 minutes.

Step 3

- At the end of the allotted time, participants compare this problem to other situations that have been solved in a collaborative way, offering empathy and suggestions.
- The group can also take this time to list proactive ideas for solving the problem.
- This discussion should last 5 to 10 minutes.

Step 4

- The facilitator asks the presenting participant to consider the information that has been provided and to explain what he or she thinks might be the most effective way to solve the problem.
- This portion of the discussion should last 10 to 20 minutes.

Step 5

- The facilitator checks with the presenting participant to see if he or she feels that the group has spent enough time on his or her behalf.
- The group debriefs the process, noting any changes they would like to make in the future.
- This process should last 5 to 10 minutes.

Silhouette Protocol

In order for students to do well in school, teachers must know their learning preferences and how they learn best. This protocol provides a structure for looking at student work and determining ways to support and meet learners' needs in order to boost their achievement. It helps teachers identify problems or areas of concern, diagnose student strengths, and focus on specific strategies for helping individual learners.

For this protocol, teachers bring the work of a student about whom they are concerned to a group meeting. Group members review the work, offer constructive feedback, and ask clarifying questions. The questions and feedback give teachers ideas for intervening, supporting, and monitoring their students' academic and emotional development. This protocol can also be used to improve teaching practice or to assist students in setting personal and academic goals.

Number of Participants: small groups of one teacher who has student work to review and no more than four participants reviewing the student work. For example, a group of 30 teachers in a PLC will work in subgroups of five; one subgroup member will present student work or a behavior record, and the remaining four members will review the work or record and provide intervention suggestions.

Required Time: 1.5 hours

A facilitator is chosen prior to the session. This individual explains the protocol, keeps track of time, and guides reflection and analysis.

Step 1—Exchange and Review

- Participants are provided with student work by the presenting educator. They look carefully at it.
- Each participant looks at three pieces of work by one student.
  - They record what they notice that the student does well.
  - They look for misconceptions about content or skills that are revealed by the student's work.
- This process lasts 10 to 15 minutes.

Step 2—Discussion

- Participants make a diagnosis about the student based on their observations of the student's work.

- Participants provide feedback to the presenting teacher about the student.
- Participants ask the teacher clarifying questions about the problem the student is having.
- Participants provide the teacher with ideas for interventions for the student.
- The presenting teacher collects the student work and asks clarifying questions of participants.

Step 3—Individual Reflection

- Participants write in journals to reflect on the suggestion or strategy that might be most effective for the student whose work the group has reviewed.

Step 4—Planning

- Participants plan for what they will do next with each of the students whose work they have reviewed.

Step 5—Debriefing

- Participants discuss what went well.
- Participants set date and time for next meeting.

Symphony

Think about a symphony. Many instruments play at their own special time, and their talents add to the wonderful piece of music. This protocol is based on the same philosophy: many students sharing their ideas in a flowing, efficient manner. Sometimes the music gets louder; at times, softer; but the end product should be a wonderful composition of shared thoughts.

Number of Participants: 20 or fewer

Required Time: no more than 20 minutes

Materials: text that has already been read by students or text that teacher has read to students

Rules

1. Participants begin a conversation that must relate to the text.

2. One speaker at a time may share a thought or idea.

3. After someone is finished speaking, the next speaker tries to add to the idea just shared.

4. Follow up ideas with "because" statements or examples from the text.

5. If the ideas shared are getting to be exhausted, you may politely say, "I'd like to take this conversation in another direction" and do so. Be sure you have an idea to share that will begin another discussion.

6. Each symphony should last at least 5 minutes.

7. Debriefing occurs.

Partner Talk

Number of Participants: no more than 25

Required Time: 20 to 40 minutes

Materials: list of discussion topics, copy of protocol guidelines, timer

Steps

1. Participants establish partnerships.

2. A facilitator may model or practice the procedure with a colleague if necessary.

3. Partners take turns speaking, following the steps in the table that follows:

Speaker A Responsibility	Speaker B Responsibility
1. Reads or talks for 5 minutes 3. After speaker B responds, discusses familiar or confusing material	2. When time is called, summarizes what speaker A read or discussed.
5. When time is called, summarizes what speaker B discussed or read.	4. Reads or talks for 5 minutes 6. After speaker A responds, discusses familiar or confusing material

Another idea similar to "Partner Talk" can be used to summarize what has been learned from a reading, video, class presentation, or discussion.

Speaker A Responsibility	Speaker B Responsibility
1. Recounts something from a reading, speaking for 60 seconds, without partner B interrupting.	2. Speaks for 60 seconds, piggy-backing upon what partner A said, adding more information, and trying not to repeat speaker A's ideas.
3. Continues discussion for 40 more seconds, trying not to repeat Partner B's ideas.	4. Continues the discussion for 40 seconds with minimal repeats.
5. Concludes discussion in 20 seconds.	6. Concludes discussion in 20 seconds.

Talking Points

This protocol provides a format for discussion of a short, nonfiction text.

Number of Participants: no more than 25

Required Time: 20 to 40 minutes

Materials: one large sticky note per participant, torn or cut into three to five strips, depending on the length of the reading

Steps

1. Participants read the text independently.

2. As they read, participants place sticky notes near information to which they respond (surprising, puzzling, exciting, etc.).

3. Participants find partners or join a small group to discuss tagged selections.

Speaker Responsibility	Partner or Group Responsibility
Summarize tagged selection.	Review own tagged selections to take note of similarities and differences.
Provide reasons why selection was chosen, referring to text when necessary.	Take turns responding to speaker, using "because" statements.
Group discusses any further reactions to text. If the conversation does not create a natural segue to another participant's tagged selection, speaker may then choose a group member to share a selection.	

4. Participants reconvene as a whole group to share their own responses or share what a group member selected.

Walk and Talk

Due to time constraints, teachers rarely have the opportunity for collegial conversations. Often frustration, lack of time, and paperwork prevent educators from making connections and bonding. "Walk and Talk" offers teachers a quick way to engage in collegial conversations about themselves or to share teaching ideas with peers.

Number of Participants: no more than 25

Required Time: 1 hour

A facilitator explains the strategy to peers and keeps track of time.

Step 1

Participants take 2 or 3 minutes to think about one of the following topics:

- Something they do well
- Who they might trade lives with if given the chance
- A lesson
- An assessment
- A classroom management technique
- An experiment
- An interaction that went well

Step 2

After the think time, participants take a few minutes to jot down thoughts related to the topic.

Step 3

- Participants form partnerships. To encourage development of new relationships, pairs can be formed using a deck of cards. For this first partner, participants can find someone who is holding a card of the same suit. With their partners, participants each take 5 minutes to share the topic they pondered during the think time.
- Participants refer to their cards again, and each finds another partner, this time with the same number as theirs. They share their topics with these new partners.

- The process is repeated a third time, with participants finding new partners whose cards have the same face as theirs.

Step 4

After the final round, participants return to their original seats and share with tablemates something new they learned about their peers.

Step 5

The facilitator leads the group in discussing the significance of this type of strategy.

Teacher Book Discussion Groups

The purpose of "Teacher Book Discussion Groups" is for teachers to gather in groups large and small to read, discuss, and reflect. This protocol was first introduced in 2000 via Laura Robb's book *Redefining Staff Development: A Collaborative Model for Teachers and Administrators*. Her belief, as ours, is that educators learn best when they have opportunities for self-directed, reflective, and inquiry-based conversations.

Number of Participants: 20 to 30

Required Time: 1 hour

Times should be set for book discussions in advance and a facilitator chosen. A sign-up sheet may be posted in the office area, or teachers may hold discussions during grade-level meeting times or lunch.

The Initial Session

- During the first meeting, participants share the names of two books they have read within the past year.
- Participants take turns providing the title of the text and a brief overview.
- The facilitator records the title of each book and makes brief notes.

Before the Next Session

- The facilitator provides participants with copies of the list.
- Participants read a book from the list or another one of their choice.

Following Sessions

- At the beginning of each session, the facilitator provides prompts the participants will use to discuss the books they have read in the interim. Examples include the following:
  - When you initially began reading the text, what were you thinking?
  - What most impressed you about the text?
  - If you could lift a line from the text, what would it be?
  - What did you notice about the author's style?

- Participants share the names of more books. This helps teachers build a list of literature from varied genres and engage in conversations about literature that can be applied to their teaching.
- For some sessions, participants can bring topics related to the text to discuss.

Ending the Session

- Prior to ending the book discussion, participants discuss new ideas or knowledge gained during the dialogue.
- Participants decide on a date and time for the next book discussion at the end of the meeting.

Teacher to Teacher Walk-Through Protocol

The "Teacher to Teacher Walk-Through" protocol can be a very powerful tool, impacting both teachers and students. The benefits for teachers include newly gained strategies, collegial conversations, and feeling safe to share concerns or try something new. Students profit as a result of improved instruction and more effective lesson delivery. The "Teacher to Teacher Walk-Through" provides a framework whereby groups of teachers can observe each other conduct live lessons in their classrooms or model new lessons they plan to deliver to students at a later date. Differentiated coaching (Kise, 2006) is at the heart of this protocol, as it takes into consideration the varied teaching and learning preferences of educators.

Number of Participants: small groups

Required Time: 15 minutes to view the lesson or demonstration, 1 hour for debriefing and collaborating as needed

ROLES OF PARTICIPANTS

The *facilitator* is selected prior to the session. This individual helps arrange and schedule each lesson or demonstration and debriefing and provides a copy of the T-chart (see Appendix A) template to participants. During the protocol, the facilitator acts as time keeper and helps guide participants in reflection and planning. After the lesson, the facilitator arranges time for the follow-up meeting.

The presenter volunteers to teach or demonstrate a lesson that will be used in the classroom. The lesson may be introducing a new concept or improving upon one already taught. Before the demonstration, the presenter provides participants with an overview or summary of the demonstration or lesson and chooses a focus question that he or she would like answered. At the time of the demonstration, the presenter introduces any students present to participants and conducts the lesson (20 minutes).

Participants who will observe the lesson review with the facilitator beforehand any pertinent information provided by the presenter. They arrive at the room where the demonstration will take place in a timely fashion, and sit quietly until there is an appropriate opportunity to interact with students. Then they ask students questions about the lesson that will help them provide appropriate feedback to the presenter. Questions may include the following:

- What are you learning today?
- What can you tell me about the work you are doing?
- How will what you are working on today help you with math [science] [reading]?

Participants use the T-chart to make notations. They write what they notice during the lesson in order to assist the presenter in analysis, revision, or further development of the lesson or to answer a question raised by the presenter. After the lesson, they meet with the presenter within 24 hours to offer feedback by reviewing, providing analysis, or asking clarifying questions.

THE FOLLOW-UP MEETING

Step 1—Introduction

- The facilitator reminds participants of the steps to the protocol, and begins the follow-up session by asking participants to silently review their notes from the lesson.

Step 2—The Protocol

- The presenter shares his or her feelings regarding the outcomes of the lesson (5 minutes).
- The presenter describes the areas or the format of the lesson that he or she would like to adjust (5 minutes).
- The facilitator calls upon participants to provide feedback in the form of questions that will allow the presenter to analyze more in depth (5 to 10 minutes). Participants should consider using questions similar to the ones that follow:
  o How do you feel about how well your lesson went? You must feel really good about the student engagement. (Praise—say something positive about what went well during the lesson, such as the tone, student engagement, clarity of directions, etc.)
  o Can you tell me more about . . . ? (clarify)
  o If you could add . . . change . . . ?
  o Do the students . . . ?
  o Would you like to collaborate on . . . ?
  o Would you consider . . . ?

Step 3—Debriefing

- The presenter speaks to the group about whether the questions were answered and whether the information he or she received was helpful (1 to 2 minutes).
- Participants discuss the value of this protocol and how they can continue to use it for reflecting in a natural way (5 minutes).
- Participants set a time and date for future discussions and planning (2 minutes).

Tools of the Trade Protocol

This protocol will assist teachers in creating and developing tools for gathering information, monitoring student growth, and evaluating the effectiveness of their teaching. The "Tools of the Trade" protocol is an efficient way to streamline resources when funds are limited. It also empowers teachers and increases collegiality. The protocol begins with teachers looking at student work and noticing trends over time. It is followed by members of the PLC gathering and listing instructional strategies and interventions that have been effective. Next, teachers spend time collecting and developing strategies and tools that will support the learning needs of the students. Finally the teachers implement the strategies and monitor and adjust as needed.

Number of Participants: small groups

Required Time: 1 to 3 years. It typically requires additional funding from a source such as the Department of Curriculum or Title 1 for an outside consultant. Participants might also enlist the aid of the district data person, administrator, or guidance counselor.

Step 1—Initiation

The facilitator

- is selected prior to the first session to work with the consultant on scheduling and logistics.
- provides a copy of a tools template to participants. (A T-chart works well for this part of the strategy; there is also a sample template in Appendix A.)

Step 2—Gathering Information

The consultant or group leader

- begins by looking at student work with participants.
- directs conversations regarding noticeable trends in the student work, what the student has done, and what still needs to be addressed.
- guides participants in listing noticeable trends, and facilitates a discussion about the monitoring tools that are in place.
- directs a recorder to list on a chart trends in student work and intervention or monitoring tools that are already in place.

Next, over a span of five to ten meetings taking place over several months, the consultant or group leader provides time for the group to research and begin developing tools of the trade that might support intervention and monitor student progress.

Step 3—Evaluation and Implementation

Participants

- use the tool that is provided by the consultant or group leader to individually list interventions and tools that are in place.
- work with the consultant or group leader to weed out tools and strategies that have not been helpful.
- meet with their colleagues to research and begin developing tools of the trade that might support intervention and monitor student progress. (This portion of the work can last several months.)
- implement the strategies, and monitor and adjust as needed.

Step 4—Sharing and Modification

The consultant or group leader

- reminds observing teachers of the last work that they completed together.
- develops common ground with a group activator.
- begins the session by randomly grouping teachers in order for them to review the work that they have accomplished and implemented.
- encourages groups to consider whether modifications are needed.
- allows time for each group to share out.
- begins conversation with the group about next steps.

Step 5—Debriefing

Participants

- determine the usefulness and effectiveness of the protocol used.
- share how the experience impacted the students with whom they work.
- consider questions or concerns that arose during the implementation process.
- consider the format for sharing the information and tools that have been developed.

Step 5—Reflection

Participants

- reflect on the experience by writing in their journals.

Give One Get One

There are many versions of this activity; however, in order to process a chunk of information, this adaptation of "Give One Get One" works well.

Number of Participants: 20 to 25

Required Time: 15 to 20 minutes

Step 1

Have the participants review what they have most recently learned. It could be something from the current day, week, or unit. Give them a few minutes to choose three highlights or important points from the material and write them on the front of an index card.

Step 2

At your signal, have participants take their pencils and index cards in hand and begin to circulate around the room to find a processing partner. They keep moving until you stop the music, ring a bell, or otherwise get them to mix up a bit. They then choose a close person to be their first partner.

Step 3

The first partner (Partner 1 of each pair) reads aloud one of the three points from his index card. The opposite member (Partner 2 of each pair) reads through her card to determine whether there is anything on the card that matches the statement Partner 1 read.

- If there is not, Partner 1 writes his statement on the back of Partner 2's index card, thus giving Partner 2 a new fact.
- If Partner 2 already had something on her card that was close to what Partner 1 read, Partner 1 reads the next statement on his card, in an attempt to find something new for his partner.

Step 4

The reader switches: Partner 2 reads aloud one of the statements on her card. Partner 1 compares it with the statements on his card. Partner 2 writes her statement on the back of Partner 1's card if he has not already written it on the front. Before you direct the partners to move again, they should each have three statements that they found themselves and one new statement on their cards.

Step 5

After a few moments of mixing, stop the group again, have them find a second partner, and once again, "give one, get one." Repeat the cycle a third time before you have the participants return to their seats.

Step 6

Debrief with the participants. Let them share what they heard most often, what they remember best, and what they were surprised to hear at all. You have a chance now to reteach and clear up any misconceptions or statements that were not correct. Music played in the background is helpful and encouraging to the task.

Kid Watching Ideas

The "Kid Watching" template in Appendix A provides a framework for watching a student interact academically, socially, or emotionally with other students or with educational experiences in the classroom setting. It is not meant to be an end-all product but is instead a quick anecdotal note-taking template to remind you of ongoing progress. Edit and revise it to fit your own classroom experiences.

Some other ideas you may consider are the following:

- Watch student working alone, in groups, and in whole group instruction.
- In a one-on-one interview with a student, ask the student to explain his or her work, draw an example, think of a rule that applies, or think of a situation in real life that could be used to exemplify the answer to a problem or concept being taught.
- Ask students to think aloud to explain what is in their heads as they talk through what they are doing. Record their thoughts.
- Use one-on-one conferences that center around reading, writing, science lab work or other content areas, or goal setting. During the conference, ask students to read their work aloud, share what their current goals may be, and indicate how their work is moving forward and what needs to happen to make the learning occur.
- Ask students to score their work based on a scoring guide. Based on the guide and class benchmarks, have students set short- and long-term goals in order to complete the assignment at a high level. Have one-minute quick conferences with individual students daily or every two days as they work toward their assessment goals. Have students use minirubrics to guide their work and record anecdotal notes in their individual student folders. (Students keep folders with notes so that they can keep track of where they are in the progress of their work.)

Ticket Into Class

Determine the question to pose on the ticket by asking yourself, "As a result of this lesson, what one question should students be able to answer to prove they understand the big idea?"

Write the question on the student tickets. At the beginning of class, distribute the tickets and explain the directions to the students. The directions should require students to write or do something that shows they understand the big idea.

Give the students time to complete their tickets.

After collecting the tickets, review them and use the data to guide future instruction and grouping.

Differentiation of Instruction Walk-Through Checklist Activities

Exit Ticket

Before students leave the classroom, they write an answer to a question or prompt about something they learned in the day's lesson.

Yesterday's News

As students enter the classroom, they write a synopsis of the previous day's lesson.

Take a Stand

The teacher creates questions related to the topic for students to discuss in small groups. Students take a stand, articulating reasons for and supporting their choices.

Reflect and Retell

Students read an assigned work, take notes, and later use their notes to aid them in retelling what was in the assigned text.

Appendix C

Resources

DIFFERENTIATED INSTRUCTION

Brimijoin, K., & Smith, N. (2005). *Differentiated instruction: Beginning the journey.* Workbook from March 2005 preconference session. Alexandria, VA: Association for Supervision and Curriculum Development.

Bromley, K. D. (1998). *Language art: Exploring connections.* Needham Heights, MA: Allyn & Bacon.

Chapman, C., & King, R. (2005*). Differentiated assessment strategies: One tool doesn't fit all.* Thousand Oaks, CA: Corwin.

Dewey, J. (1938). *Experience and education.* New York, NY: Macmillan.

Gardner, H. (1993). *Multiple intelligences: The theory in practice.* New York, NY: Basic Books.

Georgia Department of Education. (2001). *Keys to quality.* http://public.doe.k12.ga.us/tss_school.aspx

Gregory, G. H. (2005). *Differentiating instruction with style: Aligning teacher and learner intelligences for maximum achievement.* Thousand Oaks, CA: Corwin.

Gregory, G. H., & Chapman, C. (2002). *Differentiated instructional strategies: one size doesn't fit all.* Thousand Oaks, CA: Corwin.

Gregory, G. H., & Kuzmich, L. (2004). *Data driven differentiation in the standards-based classroom.* Thousand Oaks, CA: Corwin.

Gregory, G. H., & Kuzmich, L. (2005). *Differentiated literacy strategies for student growth and achievement in grades K–6.* Thousand Oaks, CA: Corwin.

Jensen, E., & Nickelsen, L. (2008). *Deeper learning.* Thousand Oaks, CA: Corwin.

Lawrence-Brown, C. (2004). Differentiated instruction: Inclusive strategies for standards-based learning that benefit the whole class. *American Secondary Education, 32*(3), 34–62.

Maslow, A. (1954). *Motivation and personality.* New York, NY: Harper & Row.

National Center on Accessing the General Curriculum (NCAC). (2000). *Differentiating curriculum: Effective practices report.* Washington, DC: U.S. Department of Education.

Northey, S. (2005). *Handbook on differentiated instruction for middle and high schools.* Larchmont, NY: Eye On Education.

Pettig, K. L. (2000). On the road to differentiated practice. *Educational Leadership, 8*(1), 14–18.

Roberts, J. L., & Inman, T. F. (2007). *Strategies for differentiating instruction: Best practices for the classroom.* Waco, TX: Prufrock.

Silver, D. (2005). *Drumming to the beat of different marchers: Finding the rhythm for differentiated learning.* Nashville, TN: Incentive.

Sizer, T. R. (2001). No two are quite alike: Personalized learning. *Educational Leadership, 57*(1), 6–11.

Strong, R. W., Silver, H. F., & Perini, M. J. (2001). *Teaching what matters most: Standards and strategies for raising student achievement.* Alexandria, VA: Association for Supervision and Curriculum Development.

Tomlinson, C. A. (1995). *How to differentiate instruction in mixed-ability classrooms.* Alexandria, VA: Association for Supervision and Curriculum Development.

Tomlinson, C. A. (1999). *The differentiated classroom: Responding to the needs of all learners.* Alexandria, VA: Association for Supervision and Curriculum Development.

Tomlinson, C. A. (1999). Mapping a route towards differentiated instruction. *Educational Leadership, 57*(1), 12–16.

Tomlinson, C. A. (2003). Differentiating instruction for academic diversity. In J. M. Cooper (Ed.), *Classroom teaching skills* (7th ed., pp. 149–180). Boston, MA: Houghton Mifflin.

Tomlinson, C. A. (2003). *Fulfilling the promise of the differentiated classroom.* Alexandria, VA: Association for Supervision and Curriculum Development.

Tomlinson, C. A., & Allan, S. D. (2000). *Leadership for differentiating schools and classrooms.* Alexandria, VA: Association for Supervision and Curriculum Development.

Tomlinson, C. A., Brighton, C., Hertberg, H., Callahan, C., Moon, T., Brimijoin, K., Conover, L., et al. (2004). Differentiating instruction in response to student readiness, interest, and learning profile in academically diverse classrooms: A review of literature. *Journal for the Education of the Gifted, 27*(2/3), 119–145.

Tomlinson, C. A., & Eidson, C. C. (2003). *Differentiation in practice: A resource guide for differentiating curriculum, grades K–5.* Alexandria, VA: Association for Supervision and Curriculum Development.

Tomlinson, C. A., & Eidson, C. C. (2003). *Differentiation in practice: A resource guide for differentiating curriculum, grades 6–12.* Alexandria, VA: Association for Supervision and Curriculum Development.

Tomlinson, C. A., & McTighe, J. (2006). *Integrating differentiated instruction & understanding by design: Connecting content and kids.* Alexandria, VA: Association for Supervision and Curriculum Development.

Tomlinson, C., & Strickland, C. (2005). *Differentiation in practice: A resource guide for differentiating curriculum, grades 9–12.* Alexandria, VA: Association for Supervision and Curriculum Development.

Villa, R., & Thousand, J. (2005). *Creating an inclusive school* (2nd ed.). Alexandria, VA: Association for Supervision and Curriculum Development.

Wiggins, G., & McTighe, J. (1998). *Understanding by design.* Alexandria, VA: Association for Supervision and Curriculum Development.

Willis, S., & Mann, L. (2000, Winter). *Differentiating instruction: Finding manageable ways to meet individual needs.* Curriculum update. Alexandria, VA: Association for Supervision and Curriculum Development.

Brain Research

Jensen, E. (2005). *Teaching with the brain in mind* (2nd ed.). Alexandria, VA: Association for Supervision and Curriculum Development.
Sousa, D. A. (2006). *How the brain learns* (3rd ed.) Thousand Oaks, CA: Corwin.
Wolfe, P. (2001). *Brain matters: Translating the research to classroom practice.* Alexandria, VA: Association for Supervision and Curriculum Development.

Cooperative Learning

Kagan, L., Kagan, M., & Kagan, S. (1997). *Cooperative learning structures for team-building.* San Clemente, CA: Kagan.
Kagan, S., & Kagan, M. (2009). *Cooperative learning.* San Clemente, CA: Kagan.

Multiple Intelligences

Campbell, L., & Campbell, B. (2008). *Mindful learning: 101 proven strategies for student and teacher success.* Thousand Oaks, CA: Corwin.
Campbell, L., Campbell, B., & Dickinson, D. (2004). *Teaching and learning through multiple intelligences* (3rd ed.). Boston, MA: Allyn & Bacon.
Fogarty, R. J., & Stoehr, J. (2008). *Integrating curricula with multiple intelligences: Teams, themes, and threads* (2nd ed.). Thousand Oaks, CA: Corwin.

Higher-Order Thinking Skills

Costa, A. (Ed.). (2009). *Habits of mind across the curriculum: Practical and creative strategies for teachers.* Alexandria, VA: Association for Supervision and Curriculum Development.
De Bono, E. (1992). *Six thinking hats for schools.* Teacher's resource books 1–4. Cheltenham, Victoria, Australia: Hawker Brownlow.

Effective Teaching

Marzano, R., Pickering, D., Arredondo, D., Blackburn, G., Brandt, R., & Moffett, C. (1992). *Dimensions of learning.* Alexandria, VA: Association for Supervision and Curriculum Development.
Marzano, R., Pickering, D., & Pollock, J. (2001). *Classroom instruction that works: Research-based strategies for increasing student achievement.* Alexandria, VA: Association for Supervision and Curriculum Development.

National Reading Panel Approaches

National Reading Panel. (2001). *Put reading first: The research building blocks for teaching children to read.* Available from http://lincs.ed.gov/publications/html/prfteachers/reading_first1.html

Organizations and Web Resources

- Annenberg Institute for School Reform, http://www.annenberginstitute.org, http://www.learner.org
- Association for Supervision and Curriculum Development, http://www.ascd.org
- Coalition of Essential Schools, http://www.essentialschools.org/
- The Council for Exceptional Children, http://www.cec.sped.org
- The National Association for Gifted Children, http://www.nagc.org

RESPONSE TO INTERVENTION

Blankstein, A. M., Cole, R. W., & Houston, P. D. (Eds.). (2007). *Engaging EVERY learner.* Vol. 1: *The soul of educational leadership.* First in an eight-volume series. Thousand Oaks, CA: Corwin.

McCook, J. (2006). *The RTI guide: Developing and implementing a model for your school.* Horsham, PA: LRP.

Senge, P. (2000). *Schools that learn, a fifth discipline fieldbook for educators, parents, and everyone who cares about education.* New York, NY: Doubleday.

Villa, R. A., & Thousand, J. S. (2005). *Creating an inclusive school* (2nd ed.). Alexandria, VA: Association for Supervision and Curriculum Development.

Organizations

- National Center on Response to Intervention, http://www.rti4success.org
- National Research Center on Learning Disabilities, http://www.nrcld.org
- National Center for Learning Disabilities, http://www.ncld.org
- National Association of State Directors of Special Education, http://www.nasdse.org

Web Resources

- Assessment and Data Management for RTI, http://www.aimsweb.com
- Dynamic Measurement Group, http://www.dibels.org
- Federal regulations at 34 CFR Part 300, Assistance to States for the Education of Children With Disabilities, http://www.cde.ca.gov/sp/se/lr/ideareathztn.asp
- Intervention Central, http://www.interventioncentral.org
- Iris Resource Locator, http://iris.peabody.vanderbilt.edu/resources.html

- Reauthorization of the Individuals with Disabilities Education Act, PL 108–446, http://www.idea.ed.gov

PROFESSIONAL LEARNING COMMUNITIES

Corcoran, T. (1995, June). *Helping teachers teach well: Transforming professional development.* CPRE Policy Brief. Philadelphia, PA: Consortium for Policy Research in Education.

Fullan, M. (2001). *The new meaning of educational change* (3rd ed.). New York, NY: Teachers College Press.

Fullan, M., & Hargreaves, A. (1991). *What's worth fighting for in your school?* New York, NY: Teachers College Press.

Hord, S. (1992). *Facilitative leadership: The imperative for change.* Austin, TX: Southwest Educational Development Laboratory.

Hord, S. (1997). *Professional learning communities: Communities of continuous inquiry and improvement.* Austin, TX: Southwest Educational Development Laboratory.

Kise, J. (2006). *Differentiated coaching: A framework for helping teachers change.* Thousand Oaks, CA: Corwin.

Robb, L. (2000). *Redefining staff development: A collaborative model for teachers and administrators.* Portsmouth, NH: Heinemann.

Southwest Educational Development Laboratory. (1994). Staff development and change process: Cut from the same cloth. *Issues About Change, 4*(2). Retrieved from http://www.sedl.org/change/issues/issues42.html

Southwest Educational Development Laboratory. (1996). Professional learning communities: What are they and why are they important? *Issues About Change, 6*(1). Retrieved from http://www.sedl.org/change/issues/issues61.html

Web Resources

- Clearinghouse on Educational Policy and Management, http://www.eric.uoregon.edu
- National Staff Developmeent Council, Learning Forward, www.learningforward.org/standards/equity.cfm

Index

CORWIN
A SAGE Company

The Corwin logo—a raven striding across an open book—represents the union of courage and learning. Corwin is committed to improving education for all learners by publishing books and other professional development resources for those serving the field of PreK–12 education. By providing practical, hands-on materials, Corwin continues to carry out the promise of its motto: **"Helping Educators Do Their Work Better."**